D1798063

Palgrave Macmillan Studies in Banking and Financial Institutions

Series Editor
Philip Molyneux
University of Sharjah
Sharjah, United Arab Emirates

The Palgrave Macmillan Studies in Banking and Financial Institutions series is international in orientation and includes studies of banking systems in particular countries or regions as well as contemporary themes such as Islamic Banking, Financial Exclusion, Mergers and Acquisitions, Risk Management, and IT in Banking. The books focus on research and practice and include up to date and innovative studies that cover issues which impact banking systems globally.

More information about this series at
http://www.palgrave.com/gp/series/14678

Francesca Arnaboldi

Risk and Regulation in Euro Area Banks

Completing the Banking Union

Francesca Arnaboldi
Department of Law Beccaria
University of Milan
Milan, Italy

ISSN 2523-336X   ISSN 2523-3378 (electronic)
Palgrave Macmillan Studies in Banking and Financial Institutions
ISBN 978-3-030-23428-7   ISBN 978-3-030-23429-4 (eBook)
https://doi.org/10.1007/978-3-030-23429-4

© The Editor(s) (if applicable) and The Author(s), under exclusive licence to Springer Nature Switzerland AG 2019
This work is subject to copyright. All rights are solely and exclusively licensed by the Publisher, whether the whole or part of the material is concerned, specifically the rights of translation, reprinting, reuse of illustrations, recitation, broadcasting, reproduction on microfilms or in any other physical way, and transmission or information storage and retrieval, electronic adaptation, computer software, or by similar or dissimilar methodology now known or hereafter developed.
The use of general descriptive names, registered names, trademarks, service marks, etc. in this publication does not imply, even in the absence of a specific statement, that such names are exempt from the relevant protective laws and regulations and therefore free for general use.
The publisher, the authors and the editors are safe to assume that the advice and information in this book are believed to be true and accurate at the date of publication. Neither the publisher nor the authors or the editors give a warranty, express or implied, with respect to the material contained herein or for any errors or omissions that may have been made. The publisher remains neutral with regard to jurisdictional claims in published maps and institutional affiliations.

Cover illustration: © QQ7 / iStock / Getty Images Plus

This Palgrave Macmillan imprint is published by the registered company Springer Nature Switzerland AG.
The registered company address is: Gewerbestrasse 11, 6330 Cham, Switzerland

FOREWORD

Bankers and policymakers today need to re-examine the major changes experienced since the global financial crisis to help them tackle the challenges of today.

A vast process of banking regulation reform has established the main traits of the European banking union. Capital requirements have been significantly increased, a guidance on non-performing loans has been introduced and new supervisory tools have been developed such as asset quality review. But the process is still incomplete: one could just think at the third pillar of the banking union, that is the European Deposit Insurance Scheme, where no apparent progress in the legislative discussion has been made since the proposal.

Post-crisis, the costs associated with the riskier areas of activity have also intensified the policy debate concerning the role and benefits of bank business models. As a response, whilst the US regulators imposed restrictions on banks' riskier areas of activity with the Dodd Frank Act of 2010, the EU regulators have long discussed a structural reform proposal on the EU banking sector without its implementation.

The above major changes will deploy their effects on banking systems, as well as on real economies, over a long period of time. The assessment of these effects and their geneses is therefore particularly important. This book of Francesca Arnaboldi is thus very welcome, as it covers many of the issues that the Euro-area banks have faced since the global financial crisis and provides a comprehensive assessment of the process of restructuring that banks have put in place.

The relevance of the issues investigated in this book finds a strong confirmation in the focus of the European supervisory authority. The first priority of the Single Supervisory Mechanism over the last three consecutive years (2016–2018) relates to business models and profitability drivers, in addition to credit risk with a focus on non-performing loans. Business models and profitability drivers represent a priority area especially in view of protracted ultra-low/negative interest rates and also in relation to potential risks emanating from the emergence of "FinTech" and non-bank competition. Credit risk remains a key issue: a number of institutions continue to be involved in a cleaning up of their balance sheets via selling off or winding down large exposures to non-performing loans. Relatedly, in the light of the recent introduction of the accounting standard "IFRS 9 Financial Instruments", the potential impact of IFRS 9 on banks might also generate further effects on bank credit policies and risk. Finally, highly complex and opaque instruments, so-called Level 3 assets, although less under the attention of the supervisory authority in comparison to credit risk, represent another major issue driving changes in the business model of the Euro-area banks.

The following pages carefully re-examine, with the support of empirical analysis and extant references to the literature, the significant restructuring process of the Euro-area banks in response to the global financial crisis. This makes the reading of this book a very worthwhile pursuit.

Università Cattolica del Sacro Cuore   Elena Beccalli
Milan, Italy

PREFACE

Since the last financial crisis, much work has been undertaken to strengthen the ability to respond to distress in the euro area financial system. The need to improve the euro area financial structure to make it less vulnerable to crises and to deliver long-term prosperity to all its members remains as strong as ever. However, even if reforms have been enacted since the Single Resolution Mechanism was created in July 2014 as part of the Banking Union initiated in 2012, the third pillar of the Banking Union, namely a European Deposit Insurance Scheme, has not been completed yet.

This reflects a deep disagreement among euro area members on the direction that reforms should take, including between its two largest members, Germany and France. France (along with other members, such as Italy) has called for additional stabilisation and risk-sharing mechanisms as well as stronger governance and accountability at the euro area level. In contrast, Germany (along with other members, such as the Netherlands) takes the view that the problems of the euro area stem mostly from inadequate domestic policies, that additional euro area stabilisation and risk-sharing instruments could be counterproductive, and that what is really needed is tougher enforcement of fiscal rules and more market discipline.

Against this background, the book first contributes to the ongoing and relevant debate by focusing on the reasons why the euro area banking system continues to remain fragile. In particular, high stocks of non-performing loans (NPLs) in some countries, the Level 3 assets evaluation and high exposure of many banks to the debts of their own governments are among the major causes of concerns. As for NPLs, the inability of borrowers to pay back their loans was aggravated during the financial crisis and the subsequent recessions. As a result, many banks saw a build-up of NPLs in their books, and this was particularly acute in some euro area countries. As highlighted by the European Central Bank (ECB) in its Risk Assessment for 2019 report, NPLs is one of the most prominent risk drivers affecting the euro area banking system, as high levels of NPLs weigh on banks' performance and profitability and ultimately have a negative impact on banks' lending to the economy. As for market risk, the recently revised ECB manual for the asset quality review of banks broadens the scope of the fair value exposures review by including Level 3 assets, and complex and illiquid Level 2 assets to better assess risks related to bank business models focused on investment services. Finally, the high exposure of many banks to the debts of their own governments raises issues regarding their economic and financial resilience in the case of adverse shocks.

The second contribution of the book relates to the completion of the public safety net for banks, including deposit insurance, which remains primarily at the national level. This creates scope for contagion from banking sector fragility to national sovereign debt distress. Integrated financial markets require a European solution with regard to deposit insurance, overcoming disagreement among euro area members. The book moves from the legislative proposal made by the European Commission in November 2015 for introducing a European Deposit Insurance Scheme (EDIS). It investigates the system of calculating risk-based contributions to deposit insurance schemes promoted by the European Banking Authority (EBA). The aim is to assess whether concerns raised by some Member States about the burden of risk sharing and the moral hazard at the prospect of introducing an EDIS are justified.

In principle this book investigates the process of restructuring that euro area banks have been facing by presenting structural developments in the euro area and by providing a broad set of structural information from both a cross-sectional perspective, that is, different ownership structures and geographical areas, and a time perspective (Chap. 1). Banks across Europe have been through a significant restructuring process in response to weak profitability and to meet the new laws and regulations that have been approved in the wake of the financial crisis. Euro area banks have spent the last decade recovering from the global financial crisis. They have been fixing their balance sheets, adopting new regulations and exiting structurally unprofitable businesses, in a low-growth environment. While the performance of European banks has improved since 2008, the average return on capital remains low. This average covers large geographic differences: banks in some European markets have completed this restructuring process, while other markets continue to struggle.

Chapter 2 presents the first of the main issues that are still undermining euro area banking system soundness, that is, the large amount of non-performing loans on banks' balance sheets. For a number of European banks, the main focus of the restructuring work has been on cleaning up their balance sheets by selling off or winding down large non-performing loan portfolios. The new International Financial Reporting Standard (IFRS) 9, which makes it less favourable to keep NPLs on the balance sheet, has made it possible to free up internal resources. This chapter provides insights into changing regulations and introduces the role of the ECB in the field of NPL management by banks and the de-risking pattern and speed to be followed.

Since the progress that banks have made in restructuring has varied among countries—depending on the nature of the crisis in their domestic markets, the type of underlying collateral and the strength of creditors' rights—Chap. 3 investigates cross-country heterogeneity in the NPL-restructuring process, focusing on those countries with the highest NPL ratios. NPLs created by local real estate bubbles have proven easier to deal with than NPLs from corporates or small- and medium-sized enterprises (SMEs) in economies struggling for competitiveness. Restructuring loans for corporates and SMEs is typically more difficult as these counterparties are often financed by multiple banks, and therefore creditor coordination becomes more complex.

The other two main issues underlying euro area banking system fragility, namely the Level 3 assets evaluation and the high exposure of many banks to the debts of their own governments, are investigated in Chap. 4. European authorities have mainly focused on fragility from credit risks, but the global financial crisis highlighted the importance of correctly pricing highly complex and opaque instruments, to avoid risk contagion, unjustified profits and regulatory capital relief. In this respect, the crisis started a trend towards simplification and transparency, entailing a radical change in banks' business models. The home bias problem is also a key obstacle to the adoption of an EDIS, as proposed by the European Commission in late 2015, because deposits protected by this scheme might be used by banks, under moral suasion from their home country's government, to excessively increase their purchases of that government's debt. As a response to this, policymakers are now discussing whether and how to address the treatment of sovereign debt on bank balance sheets, which is currently treated as risk-free.

Chapter 5 focuses on the progress achieved and rules to be completed on the first and second pillar of the Banking Union. After the global financial crisis, the institutional and regulatory framework for European banks has been fundamentally reinforced, resulting in a substantial reduction of risks in the banking sector. Several key elements of the Banking Union are already established. The European Commission's first review of the Single Supervisory Mechanism shows that its establishment was overall successful. Risk assessments have become more harmonised and systematic, whereas, in the past, broad discretion in applying euro area rules led to significant national differences in key prudential aspects, such as the definition of funds, or capital and liquidity requirements. Nevertheless, despite having a single supervisor and more harmonised rules, the banking market in Europe remains fragmented. There are fundamental legal, judicial and cultural differences among countries, which are obstacles to cross-border integration.

In addition to this, Chap. 6 examines the missing piece to the Banking Union, that is the single EDIS. Following the European Commission's proposal in 2015, a number of different recommendations have arisen in this area, but none of these options has met sufficient consensus among euro area countries, producing a deadlock in the policy discussion, with no apparent progress in the legislative discussion of the 2015 proposal itself. This chapter investigates the evolution of the third pillar after the approval of Directive 2014/49/EU.

Finally, Chap. 7 empirically investigates the level of contribution banks must provide to a single deposit insurance scheme (DIS) according to their level of risk. European Banking Authority (EBA) guidelines on methods for calculating contributions to DISs are applied to a sample of global systemically significant banks in two different points in time: in 2014, before the Commission's proposal on an EDIS, and in 2018, the last year with available accounting data on the EBA website. For the banks under scrutiny, core and additional indicators, as defined by the EBA, are computed. Indicators belong to one of the following risk categories: capital; liquidity and funding; asset quality; business model and management; and potential losses for the DIS. The aim of this empirical investigation is to contribute to the regulatory debate by assessing which countries—if any—are better off after the full implementation of common monitoring systems of bank riskiness.

This book combines an in-depth analysis of the regulatory framework and empirical investigation on euro area banking system data to prove that market discipline and risk sharing should be viewed as complementary pillars of the euro area financial architecture, rather than as substitutes. Achieving this complementarity, however, is not easy. It calls for stabilisation and insurance mechanisms that are both effective and cannot give rise to permanent transfers and it requires further reforms of the institutional framework.

Milan, Italy   Francesca Arnaboldi

ACKNOWLEDGEMENTS

The author would like to thank the series editor Philip Molyneux, four anonymous referees, E. Beccalli, C. Bisoni, B. Rossignoli and E. Miklaszewska (discussant), and the participants at the 2016 HEC roundtable at HEC Montreal, Canada; at the 2016 Wolpertinger Conference at Università di Verona, Italy, and at the 2018 Seminar on The Regulation of Financial Markets in Europe at the Université de Montréal, Canada, for their insightful and constructive comments. Any errors are my own.

This work forms part of an ongoing research project on "Dove va l'Europa? Percorsi e prospettive del federalizing process europeo". The author gratefully acknowledges financial support from PRIN 2017— Progetti di Rilevanza Nazionale, Ministero dell'Istruzione, dell'Università e della Ricerca, Italian Government.

CONTENTS

LIST OF FIGURES

LIST OF TABLES

CHAPTER 1

The Euro Area Banking System: Where Do We Stand?

1.1 Introduction

Banks across Europe have been through a significant restructuring process in response to weak profitability and to meet the new laws and regulations that have been approved in the wake of the financial crisis. Euro area banks have spent the last decade recovering from the global financial crisis. They have been fixing their balance sheets, adopting new regulations and exiting structurally unprofitable businesses in a low-growth environment. While the performance of European banks has improved since 2008, the average return on capital is still low. This average covers large geographic differences: banks in some European markets have completed this restructuring process, while other markets continue to struggle. First, the chapter analyses the process of restructuring that euro area banks have been facing. Then it investigates the European banking system, presenting structural developments in the euro area, providing a broad set of structural information from both a cross-sectional perspective, that is, different ownership structures and geographical areas, and a time perspective, and setting the context for the investigation on nonperforming loans (NPLs) in Chap. 2.

© The Author(s) 2019   1
F. Arnaboldi, *Risk and Regulation in Euro Area Banks*, Palgrave
Macmillan Studies in Banking and Financial Institutions,
https://doi.org/10.1007/978-3-030-23429-4_1

1.2   EURO AREA BANKING SYSTEM
RESTRUCTURING PROCESS

Much has been done in the past ten years to enhance the resilience of the euro area banking sector. A sample formed by all banking groups in the European Central Bank (ECB) supervisory reporting framework indicates that the performance of euro area banks has recovered from 2008 (Fig. 1.1). Both the return on equity and return on assets of domestic banking groups and stand-alone banks have increased over the last decade.

The average return on equity in 2017 was 6.2 per cent, compared to 0.4 per cent in 2008. Figure 1.2 presents data for the return on assets for euro area banks. The picture is quite similar, with the average return on assets being 0.6 per cent in 2017, which was double the 0.3 per cent of 2008.

The process of restructuring varies with country, but most banks are now nearing completion of their efforts to close unprofitable lines of business, reduce the stock of non-performing loans on their balance sheet and meet the higher capital requirements and liquidity ratios. Despite this progress, profitability is still below the hurdle rate for many banks. In some countries, such as Cyprus, Greece and Portugal, the average return on equity is still negative.

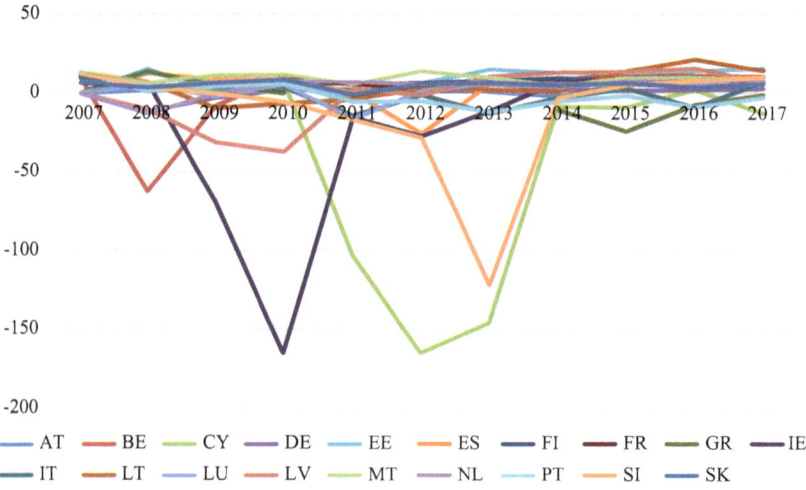

Fig. 1.1   Return on equity euro area domestic banking groups and stand-alone banks (%). Source: Author's elaboration on ECB (2018c)

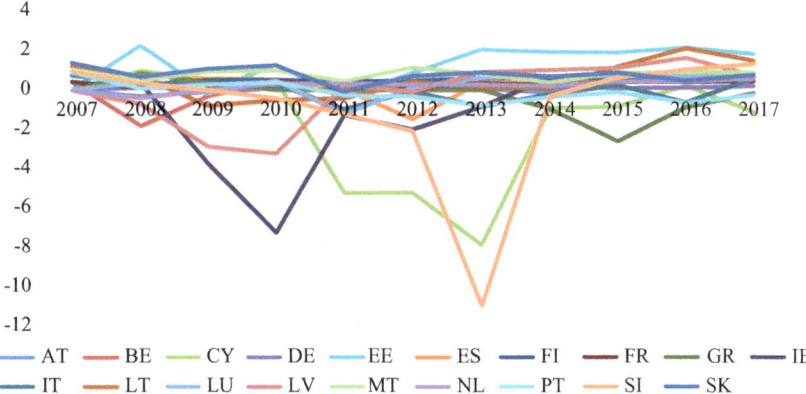

Fig. 1.2 Return on assets euro area domestic banking groups and stand-alone banks (%). Source: Author's elaboration on ECB (2018c)

The European Central Bank has indicated that low bank profitability is one of the key systemic risks to euro area financial stability (ECB 2018b). Low profitability *leaves banks vulnerable to a possible turnaround in the business cycle*. The ability to generate adequate profits is a key element for banks to avoid losing shareholders, diminishing market capitalisation and gradually decreasing their solvency. In other words, a bank that is not adequately profitable cannot guarantee its sustainability over time. The low profitability issue and the need for euro area banks to adjust their business models have also been highlighted by the ECB and the International Monetary Fund (IMF) in recent publications (ECB 2018d; IMF 2018). The introduction of stricter capital and liquidity requirements, which is described in the next chapters, and the higher compliance costs associated to the new regulatory framework, inevitably affects the ability of banks to being profitable (Sironi 2018).

Profitability differs across institutions like the ability to face a changing environment. Not all banks are affected to the same extent: the evolution of banks' core banking revenues varies substantially. For example, from a sample of 380 euro area commercial banks, 137 (36 per cent) managed to increase both net interest income and net fee and commission income from 2013 to 2017, while 111 (29 per cent) managed to raise core banking revenues by substituting net interest income with fee and commission income.[1] Fifty-eight banks (15 per cent) were able to increase net interest income

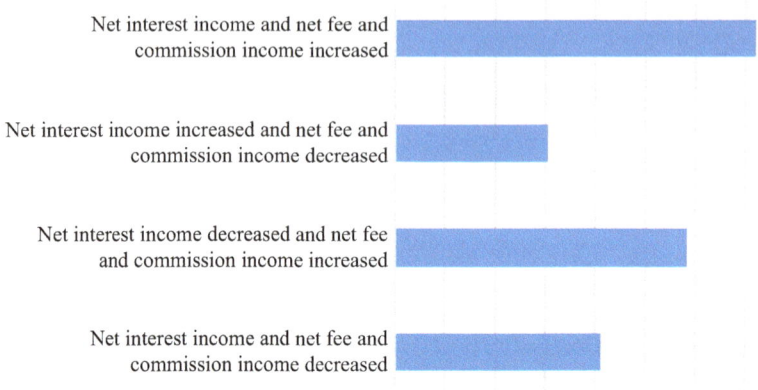

Fig. 1.3 Euro area commercial bank profitability (2013–2017). Source: Author's elaboration on Orbis Bank data

despite the low interest rates but had lower fee and commission income. Nevertheless, 78 banks (20 per cent) could not compensate for decreasing income from lending activities with other sources of income (Fig. 1.3).

At the size level, the largest banks in the sample (total assets in 2017 larger than 9.15 billion euro, top quartile of the overall sample distribution) represent the majority of banks able to raise their profit-generating capacity over the last five years by boosting both net interest income and net fee and commission income (48 out of 137 banks). By contrast, smaller banks were the majority of banks not able to generate higher revenues from fee and commission business to compensate for their large decline in net interest income from 2013 to 2017 (Fig. 1.4). A possible explanation can be found in the business model adjustment. The ECB (2016) shows that, in the past, diversified banks have been more successful in generating higher revenues from net fees and commissions and trading when faced with pressure on interest income. This is perhaps no surprise, as larger banks may engage in custodian, asset management or investment banking activities that are likely to be better able to move themselves towards fee-generating activities. Smaller banks may not have access to such opportunities for diversification.

The sample distribution by profitability and country is reported in Fig. 1.5.

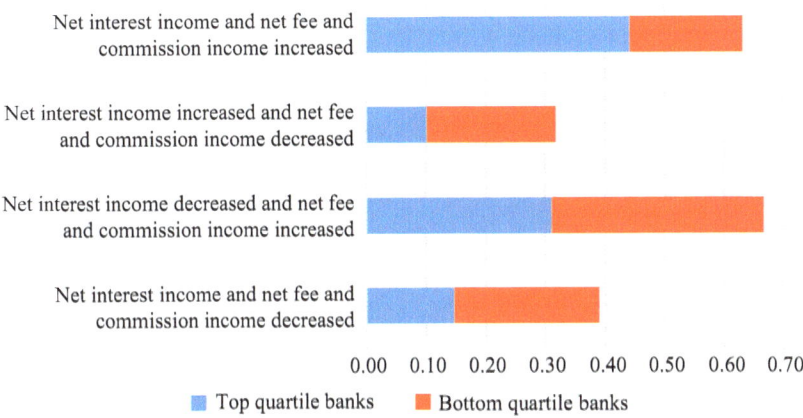

Fig. 1.4 Euro area commercial bank profitability by bank total assets (2013–2017).
Source: Author's elaboration on Orbis Bank data

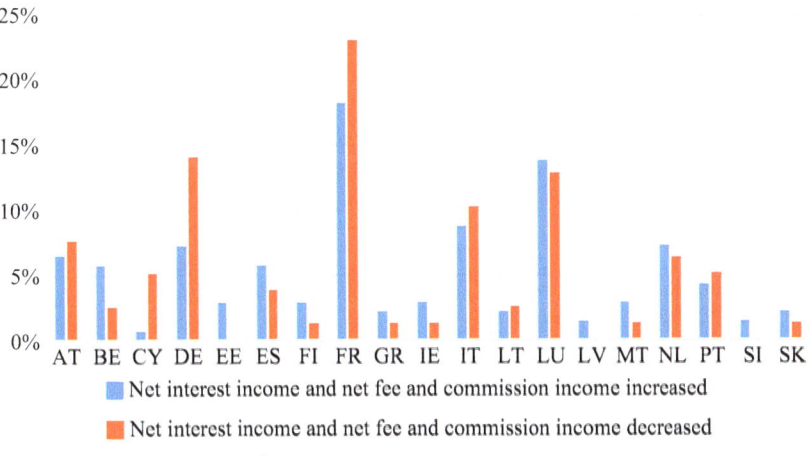

Fig. 1.5 Profitability of euro area commercial banks by country (2013–2017).
Source: Author's elaboration on Orbis Bank data

The greater number of banks not able to compensate for decreasing income from lending activities with other sources of income is in general located in the largest euro area countries, that is, in France, Germany and Italy. In contrast, banks in smaller countries, such as Belgium, Estonia,

Latvia, Slovakia and Slovenia, are able to boost both net interest income and net fee and commission income. Both cyclical and structural factors can help explain these differences. On the cyclical front, even if monetary easing ends and interest rates start to rise, this may not lead to an increase in margins. Drivers of bank growth may be difficult to find in many of the euro area's mature markets.

As for the structural challenges, digital innovations (e.g. comparison websites) and regulatory requirements, such as the transparency measures in Directive 2014/65/EU–MiFID II, enhanced price transparency. Greater price transparency may prevent banks from realising margins seen in previous high-rate environments even if cyclical factors improve.

Digital innovations and technological advances not only support greater transparency but also change the competitive landscape, thereby representing a key strategic opportunity and a challenge for banks at the same time. The impact of digital banking on cost-efficiency is examined in the next section. On the revenue side, incumbent banks face increasing competition from the non-bank financial sector and fintech firms, fuelled by the increasing role of technology in financial services. Philippon (2018) describes fintech as an industry that covers digital innovations and technology-enabled business model innovations in the financial sector. Increased competition in lending, investments and payments is likely to increase pressure on retail banking profitability and on business model adjustments. It will subject deposits to more intense price competition and may erode revenues related to overdrafts and payments (ECB 2016).

High impairments and legacy issues also contribute to low performance. Non-performing loan (NPL) stocks are decreasing in most countries; nevertheless, the current aggregate level of NPLs remains far too high by international standards.[2]

Additional challenges on the revenue side may also come from US banks and their set-up of new branches in the EU as a result of the exit of the United Kingdom from the European Union (Brexit). US banks should therefore find new sources of revenue to meet the increased cost of their EU footprint. On this note, in 2018, Goldman Sachs opened its digital consumer savings platform Marcus in the United Kingdom (Goldman Sachs 2018). Since its launch in the United States in 2016, the digital bank has accumulated more than $20 billion in deposits, as Goldman Sachs seeks to diversify its sources of funding and compete with rival US lenders that have full retail banks (Reuters 2018). The bank offers an online savings account to customers in the United Kingdom, and forms part of the bank's strategy to grow its consumer business. In principle, the US investment bank challenges incumbent UK lenders such as HSBC and Barclays, as well as start-up digital players such as Atom Bank and Tandem, which also offer savings accounts via mobile apps, but may seek to expand its consumer bank through acquisitions or buying a traditional lender in euro area countries, such as, for instance, Germany.

Another challenge is linked to the need to improve cost-efficiency, which is now examined.

1.2.1 Cost-Efficiency

Figure 1.6 shows the efforts of euro area banks in cutting costs and simplifying infrastructure since the inception of the global financial crisis.

The cost-to-income ratio decreased by 19 per cent from 72 per cent in 2008 to 58.5 per cent in 2017. Nevertheless, taking a closer look, banks' cost-efficiency has deteriorated since 2010 and empirical evidence suggests that there is substantial scope for improvements (ECB 2018b). Euro area banks' aggregate cost-to-income ratio rose from 47.6 per cent in 2010 to 58.5 per cent in 2017, primarily driven by an increase in overheads. A recent study on the euro area banks' cost-efficiency shows that long-term structural factors play a more significant role in bank cost-efficiency than cyclical factors (ECB 2018a). In particular, physical

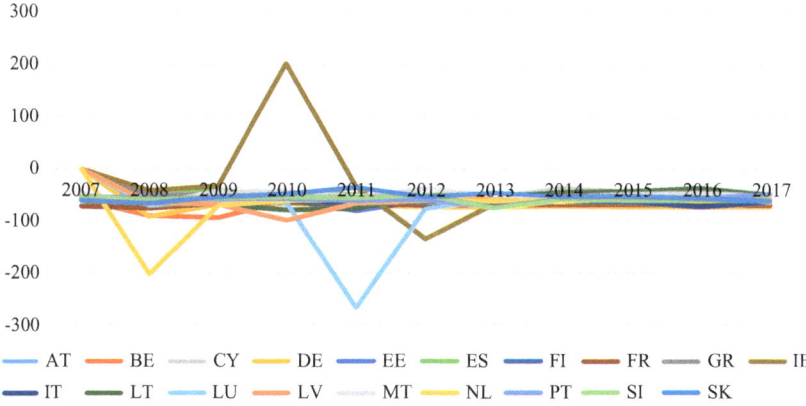

Fig. 1.6 Cost-to-income ratio euro area domestic banking groups and stand-alone banks (%). Source: Author's elaboration on ECB (2018c)

branches represent one of those factors. Among the possible measures to improve structural efficiency, digital banking and the subsequent shift away from physical branches have been indicated as a permanent cost-saving opportunity for banks. For example, a shift from branch networks towards digital banking has enabled many banks, particularly in the Nordic countries, to reduce costs while maintaining sound customer bases and market shares.

Nevertheless, physical branches may be more effective in keeping the relationship with the client than digital banking. The scope for potential cost savings via digital banking may be not as relevant as expected, especially in countries where a physical relationship between the bank and the client is important. Transformation is likely to be successful in countries that experiment with the support of beneficial structural factors such as labour laws, how the market is structured and the digital readiness of the economy. Usually these features characterise Nordic countries, which historically encouraged the digitalisation of large part of the economy. Indeed, policy action both at European and at domestic level may have a role in supporting these conditions (ECB 2016).

1.2.2   Financial Integration

Euro area banks are very heterogeneous in terms of size, scope and geographical provenance. Differences in performance and efficiency ratios remain striking among Southern and Northern euro area countries. In 2017, though the cost-to-income ratio of Southern European banks was 55.2 per cent, compared with 60.4 for Northern banks, the return on equity was 2.24 per cent compared with 8.5 per cent in the North. On top of profitability and efficiency differences, cultural, legal and language barriers may make it difficult to directly provide cross-border banking services. For example, in 2017, cross-border loans amounted to only 8.6 per cent of total loans to firms and 0.9 per cent of loans to households (ECB 2018e).

The economic benefits of an increase in cross-border banking activities include higher diversification of risks, which can improve resilience and lead to better risk-sharing across countries. Banking sector integration also matters for the good functioning of the Monetary Union, as it fosters the smooth transmission of monetary policy throughout the euro area economy.

Despite these benefits, progress in banking market integration in Europe has been slow, particularly in retail banking. Over the last decade, consolidation has taken place within many euro area retail markets, especially in countries more affected by the financial crisis. However, some markets, in particular Austria, Germany and Italy, remain fragmented (ECB 2018d). The euro area cross-border banking retrenchment was driven to a greater extent by source country factors, highlighting the spillovers from national banking sector conditions across the euro area.

Nevertheless, the current favourable macroeconomic environment and more regulatory certainty due to the finalisation of the Basel reforms, as well as improving bank fundamentals, should help mergers and acquisitions (M&A). M&A may deliver important cost savings through economies of scale, particularly in less concentrated banking markets, as has been widely debated in the literature (Berger et al. 1987; Berger and Humphrey 1991, 1992; ECB 2017; Molyneux et al. 1996; Revell 1997). However, making further progress towards the completion of the Banking Union and the capital markets union, as well as overcoming prevailing regulatory, supervisory and external obstacles, such as, for instance, the harmonisation of insolvency laws and taxation regimes, the establishment of a European Deposit Insurance Scheme (EDIS) and the subsequent removal of national options and discretions, may be necessary to facilitate larger-scale M&A within the euro area banking sector.[3] In particular, external impediments are related to political decisions which obstruct cross-country M&A. Such impediments hardly have sound economic and financial ground but nevertheless impact banks business strategies. Additionally, special attention should be paid to the emergence of potential risks associated with too-big-to-fail institutions that may result from the M&A process.

With regard to non-bank competition, the impact of fintech remains to be seen, and big tech players could enter the market and alter the landscape, in particular with the adoption of the revised Payment Services Directive (PSD2–Directive 2015/2366/EU). A number of banks are already actively pursuing partnerships with fintech companies, seeking the opportunity to increase margins and entering new markets without legacy issues. On the other hand, a range of industrial and tech companies are straying into the field of finance. At the moment, this is mostly based on payments, but it is easy to imagine how these service operators could go further and start offering loans in order to optimise the customer experience. Given their customer base, technological knowledge and solvency, these players could significantly disrupt the world of banking (ECB 2018d).

1.2.3   Challenges for Regulators

Despite progress made towards the Banking Union, euro area banks are still heterogeneous. Banks that have outperformed the others over the last few years are geographically spread out and have differing size and business models. Some banks were particularly cost-efficient, while others managed to generate significantly higher revenues (relative to their total assets) than their peers. Even strategies among the best-performing banks have largely differed with regard to costs and income. Cost reduction, however, is not a panacea: banks that reduced staff have certainly decreased expenses, but apparently have not been able to maintain income levels (ECB 2018b).

One of the main challenges for the supervisory authority is not to apply a one-size-fits-all approach, that is, to tailor the supervisory activity to the specific issues each bank faces. This is particularly challenging because a tailored approach may reduce comparability and add complexity to the system. Nevertheless, banks' strategies largely reflect their current state of profitability: weaker banks are trying to reduce their costs and NPLs, while better performers tend to focus on growth (ECB 2018b). Many banks are now planning to grow and they need to make well-informed decisions about risk-taking and make sure their strategic steering capability is commensurate with the risk of their activities. Banks that are planning to cut costs need to ensure that essential risk management and controls are not affected, that they maintain their franchise and that they keep up the necessary investments (e.g. in information technology [IT]) to be able to achieve their business goals in the long run. In this framework, one of the main tasks of the supervisory authority is to verify whether banks' plans are based on unrealistic assumptions. Unfortunately, this is not an easy task. Many assumptions are based on data quite hard to estimate: the impact of digitalisation, the market shares fintech firms are going to acquire, cost-efficiency based on regtech and the estimated impact of cyber risks are just a few examples.

A second challenge is related to completing the financial union, in particular the Banking Union, with a backstop for the Single Resolution Framework (SRF) and a credible European Deposit Insurance Scheme (EDIS), as well as the capital market union. The first two mechanisms would improve financial stability in the euro area by increasing confidence and reducing the likelihood of a bank failure (ECB 2018e). A European

Deposit Insurance Scheme would increase customers' trust, as their deposits would be reimbursed following common European rules, regardless of the country where the bank is incorporated. This would help break the link between banks and sovereigns in some countries, as is investigated in Chaps. 4 and 6. Furthermore, pooling resources at the Banking Union level would enhance the banking sector's resilience to shocks without leading to systematic transfers of risk between banking sectors. Indeed, banks' contributions to their national Deposit Insurance Funds already reflect their relative riskiness; the same structure can hold at the European level, with adjustments in terms of NPLs or sovereign exposures, for example. An EDIS would also remove the current misalignment among the three pillars of the Banking Union where supervision and resolution are regulated at the European level, while depositor protection remains a national task.

Third, developments in the non-bank financial sector also require monitoring, as the sector continues to become larger, more interconnected and more exposed to risks. Philippon (2018) shows that fintech innovations can disrupt existing industry structures and blur industry boundaries. They can create significant privacy, regulatory and law enforcement challenges. However, since the current financial system is rather inefficient and focus on incumbents inherent in current regulations increases political economy and coordination costs, the author suggests that regulators consider policies that promote low-leverage technologies and the entry of new firms, if the goal of financial regulation is to foster stability and access to services.

1.3   EURO AREA BANKING SYSTEM FACT SHEETS

As previously mentioned, the financial health of euro area banks has improved since the global financial crisis. In the previous sections, data on euro area banks' profitability and cost-efficiency have been reported. To provide a sound framework and set up the ground for the following chapters, a sample of euro area commercial banks is now considered and data from 2011 are reported (Table 1.1).[4] The sample is formed by 752 banks covering all euro area countries. The majority of the sample is formed by German and French banks (19 and 18 per cent of the sample, respectively), followed by Luxembourg, Italy and Spain (9, 8 and 7 per cent of the sample, respectively).

Table 1.1 Sample composition

Country	No. of banks	Sample (%)
Austria	41	0.05
Belgium	37	0.05
Cyprus	34	0.05
Estonia	7	0.01
Finland	36	0.05
France	136	0.18
Germany	140	0.19
Greece	7	0.01
Ireland	21	0.03
Italy	58	0.08
Latvia	15	0.02
Lithuania	6	0.01
Luxembourg	68	0.09
Malta	12	0.02
Netherlands	32	0.04
Portugal	33	0.04
Slovakia	10	0.01
Slovenia	9	0.01
Spain	50	0.07
Total	752	1.00

Source: Author's elaboration on Orbis Bank data

From 2011, banks become larger on average, with total assets increasing from 91.6 to 137 billion euro, and more profitable (Table 1.2). As previously described, euro area banks' profitability has improved in the last decade, and this is confirmed by also investigating the 2011–2018 data. The return on asset increased from 0.02 per cent in 2011 to 0.52 per cent in 2018. The average return on equity for euro area banks decreased from 18.1 per cent in 2011 to 6.7 per cent in 2018, which can be explained by the different dynamic of the ratio components. While net income improved over the period from an average 111 to 630 million euro, total equity stood at around 8.5 billion euro, double of what it was in 2011. Banks are improving their solidity, with the total capital ratio moving from 16 to 23 per cent and the tier 1 ratio from 13 to 22 per cent. The equity-to-total asset ratio confirms the improvement in solidity, increasing from 9 to 11 per cent on average. At the same time, banks rely more on customer deposits (from 34.6 to 68.9 billion euro, almost +100 per cent), which are usually considered a more stable funding base. On top of that, the liquid assets to deposit and short-term funding have decreased from 274 to 37 per cent.

While euro area banks are clearly better capitalised, this exercise should not hide the fact that areas of vulnerability remain. In particular, banks are struggling in terms of cost-efficiency, as the cost-to-income ratio increased from 63.5 per cent in 2011 to 68.2 per cent in 2018. The main driver of this is the significant increase in overheads, which almost doubled in the period under investigation (from 1.3 to 2.1 billion euro).

Sustainable profitability is also an area of concern. Even if the margin from fees and commissions improves (+51 per cent from 2011 to 2018), the net interest margin remains stable at about 2 per cent. On the cyclical front, banks are finding it hard to increase their net interest margin in the low interest rate environment. Although a more careful analysis on loans shows that the total amount of loans increased by 64 per cent with the improving economic conditions, it is not yet sufficient to compensate for the low interest rate margins. The continued economic recovery should, however, reduce the negative impact of cyclical factors over time, as banks' balance sheets adjust, not least thanks to the reduction in the cost of credit risk. Indeed, the stock of non-performing loans has decreased on average by 5.7 per cent and the NPLs-to-gross loans ratio is now 5 per cent, as compared to 8 per cent in 2011.

1.3.1   *Listed and Not Listed Banks*

Table 1.2 reports data on the whole sample of banks considered and for listed and not listed banks separately. As expected, listed banks are on average larger than not listed banks, but surprisingly less profitable in terms of return on assets. The trend in return on equity is different, as not listed banks' return on equity increased on average from 2011 to 2018, whereas listed banks' Return on Equity (ROE) sharply decreased over the same period (from 94 to 7 per cent). Both listed and not listed banks strengthened their solidity in the period as the positive change in total equity, total capital, tier 1 and equity-to-total asset ratio suggests. All banks have gone back to a more traditional banking model, funding more extensively via customer deposits (+57 and +77 per cent, respectively).

In terms of efficiency, listed banks were able to reduce the cost-to-income ratio, unlike not listed banks (−5 per cent and +13 per cent,

Table 1.2 Euro area banks descriptive statistics

	All sample mean			Listed banks mean			Not listed banks mean		
	2018	2011	Variation (%)	2018	2011	Variation (%)	2018	2011	Variation (%)
Total assets (in thousand)	137,000,000	91,600,000	0.50	306,000,000	256,000,000	0.20	50,600,000	43,900,000	0.15
Return on average asset (%)	0.52	0.02	24.37	0.10	−0.61	−1.17	0.73	0.20	2.58
Return on average equity (%)	6.68	18.09	−0.63	6.72	93.82	−0.93	6.66	−3.88	−2.72
Net income (in thousand)	629,610	−110,781	−6.68	1,333,417	−502,241	−3.65	272,453	2791	96.62
Total equity (in thousand)	8,493,431	4,309,201	0.97	18,900,000	11,900,000	0.59	3,206,614	2,107,235	0.52
Total capital ratio (%)	23.08	16.15	0.43	17.40	13.56	0.28	26.01	17.43	0.49
Tier ratio (%)	21.69	13.17	0.65	15.50	11.35	0.37	24.74	14.26	0.73
Equity-to-total asset (%)	11.01	9.43	0.17	10.89	6.55	0.66	11.07	10.26	0.08
Customer deposits (in thousand)	68,900,000	34,600,000	0.99	136,000,000	86,600,000	0.57	32,700,000	18,500,000	0.77
Liquid assets to deposit and short-term funding (%)	36.62	273.73	−0.87	28.89	23.61	0.22	40.67	348.14	−0.88
Cost to income (%)	68.20	63.53	0.07	63.34	66.57	−0.05	70.74	62.64	0.13
Overheads (in thousand)	2,114,041	1,322,208	0.60	4,862,626	3,912,183	0.24	698,103	566,129	0.23
Net interest margin (%)	2.20	1.87	0.18	1.90	2.03	−0.07	2.35	1.82	0.29
Net fees and commissions (in thousand)	767,278	507,539	0.51	1,768,690	1,522,995	0.16	235,278	211,101	0.11
Net loans (in thousand)	69,200,000	42,300,000	0.64	144,000,000	111,000,000	0.30	31,000,000	21,800,000	0.42
Non-performing loans (in thousand)	1,919,710	2,035,014	−0.06	4,397,201	4,552,190	−0.03	538,032	1,006,255	−0.47
Non-performing loans/gross loans (%)	5.03	7.85	−0.36	6.12	8.54	−0.28	4.35	7.55	−0.42

Source: Author's own elaboration on Orbis Bank data

respectively). Not listed banks better exploit the low interest rate environment, as their net interest margin increased by 30 per cent, as opposed to −7 per cent for listed banks. They probably operate in smaller, local markets where some inefficiency still remains in pricing loans. In fact, they were also able to improve the quality of their loan portfolio, by reducing the NPLs by 47 per cent, more significantly than listed banks (−3 per cent). Both groups of banks generate higher additional revenues from fees and commissions (+16 and +11 per cent for listed and not listed banks, respectively).

1.3.2 Southern and Northern Euro Area Countries

In this section, data on Southern and Northern euro area banks are presented to provide evidence of the level of heterogeneity, if any, between the two areas. Banks in the sample have been assigned to the Southern euro area group if incorporated in Cyprus, France, Greece, Italy, Malta, Portugal, Slovenia or Spain; banks in Austria, Belgium, Estonia, Finland, Germany, Ireland, Latvia, Lithuania, Luxembourg, the Netherlands or Slovakia belong to the Northern euro area group. Table 1.3 reports on the test for difference in means between the two groups for the variables of interest.[5]

Southern euro area banks were, on average, bigger than their Northern peers both in 2011 and in 2018 (Table 1.3, Panel A and Panel B). The difference in size became significant at the 5 per cent level in 2018. Northern banks were significantly more profitable in terms of average return on assets and net income in 2011, but they were less profitable in 2018. Return on equity for Southern euro area banks was much higher than for their Northern peers in 2011, whereas in 2018 the gap was almost closed.

In terms of solidity, Southern and Northern banks are significantly different: the latter had higher tier 1, total capital and equity-to-total asset ratios, both in 2011 and in 2018. In fact, the difference is larger now than it was during the sovereign debt crisis.

Funding is significantly more based on customer deposits for Southern banks, which are also more liquid and have largely improved their cost-to-income ratio as compared to Northern euro area banks (130 vs. 45.4 billion euro; 64 vs. 26 per cent; 61 vs. 71 per cent in 2018, respectively). In particular, the reduction of the cost-to-income ratio can be only partially explained by higher efficiency, as overheads are significantly higher in the

Table 1.3 Test for difference in means—Southern and Northern euro area countries

	Southern euro area countries		Northern euro area countries		Difference in means
	No. Obs	Mean	No. Obs	Mean	
Panel A—2011					
Total assets (in billion)	105	115	104	68.2	−46.8
Return on average asset (%)	105	−0.35	104	0.4	0.75***
Return on average equity (%)	105	34.60	104	1.39	−33.21
Net income (in billion)	105	−0.32	104	0.10	0.43**
Total equity (in billion)	105	5.65	104	2.96	−2.70*
Total capital ratio (%)	59	13.68	68	18.3	4.62***
Tier ratio (%)	57	12.05	47	14.52	2.47**
Equity-to-total asset (%)	105	7.57	104	11.3	3.73**
Customer deposits (in billion)	101	41.3	98	27.7	−13.6
Liquid assets to deposit and short-term funding (%)	105	27.51	100	532.27	504.76
Cost to income (%)	105	63.84	103	63.22	−0.62
Overheads (in billion)	105	1.77	103	0.87	−0.90**
Net interest margin (%)	105	2.12	103	1.61	−0.51***
Net fees and commissions (in billion)	105	0.70	103	0.31	−0.40**
Net loans (in billion)	105	54.5	100	29.6	−24.9**
Non-performing loans (in billion)	102	2.49	60	1.26	−1.23**
Non-performing loans/gross loans (%)	100	8.81	47	5.82	−2.99**
Panel B—2018					
Total assets (in billion)	27	292	74	80.1	−211.9**
Return on average asset (%)	27	0.61	74	0.48	−0.13
Return on average equity (%)	27	6.67	74	6.68	0.01
Net income (in billion)	27	1.41	74	0.34	−1.07**
Total equity (in billion)	27	17.8	74	5.09	−12.71**
Total capital ratio (%)	25	16.04	69	25.63	9.59***
Tier ratio (%)	22	14.56	63	24.19	9.63***
Equity to total asset (%)	27	8.61	74	11.89	3.28**
Customer deposits (in billion)	26	130	68	45.4	−84.6**
Liquid assets to deposit and short-term funding (%)	27	64.06	69	25.89	−38.17*
Cost to income (%)	26	60.87	73	70.81	9.94**
Overheads (in billion)	26	4.83	74	1.16	−3.67**
Net interest margin (%)	27	2.15	73	2.21	0.06
Net fees and commissions (in billion)	25	1.77	73	0.42	−1.35**
Net loans (in billion)	26	136	72	45	−91**
Non-performing loans (in billion)	21	5.53	60	0.66	−4.87***
Non-performing loans/gross loans (%)	22	9.2	53	3.31	−5.89**

Source: Author's elaboration on Orbis Bank data

Note: The table reports the summary statistics (number of observations, mean values and differences in means) for the banks' variables in 2011 and 2018. The t-statistics are calculated using standard errors clustered at the bank level are reported in parentheses. *, ** and *** indicate significance at 10%, 5% and 1% levels, respectively

South than in the North. While Northern banks managed to increase their revenue in the low interest rate environment, Southern peers had a significantly higher amount of net fees and commissions both in 2011 and in 2018, which somehow compensates for the lower interest rate margin.

Southern banks traditionally engage in lending activity, but the quality of their loan portfolio is worsening: not only was the stock of NPLs in Southern euro area banks significantly higher than in their Northern peers both in 2011 and in 2018 but also the stock more than doubled in the period under scrutiny. The non-performing loans-to-gross loans ratio further highlights the difference in credit risk. From 2011 to 2018, Northern banks were able to reduce the ratio from 5.8 per cent to 3.3 per cent, as compared to Southern banks whose ratio increased from 8.8 to 9.2 per cent.

1.4   CONCLUSION

The resilience of the euro area banking sector has increased considerably since the financial crisis. Profitability has improved, and bank solidity and regulatory liquidity ratios are at sound levels. The results of the 2018 stress tests reflect the numbers in the euro area banking system presented in this first chapter (EBA 2018). However, structural challenges and the financial stability outlook suggest that the remaining issues that are preventing the financial union from reaching its full potential should be tackled. A first area of intervention is represented by banks' business models. Further diversification may help to counterbalance low profitability, and digitalisation can help to reduce cost inefficiencies as investigated in this chapter. Chapters 2, 3 and 4 address the main areas of concern for policymakers, that is, the large stocks of NPLs that still remain in some banks, the Level 3 assets evaluation and the exposure to sovereign debt.

Second, policymakers need to maintain the momentum towards completing the financial union. Chapters 5 and 6 describe the necessary steps to complete the Banking Union and remove regulatory obstacles to cross-border banking sector consolidation. A final remark is on the completion of the capital markets union and on the advantages that can be reaped thanks to the synergies between the two unions. Chapter 7 concludes with an empirical investigation on the rules proposed by the European Banking Authority to further reduce national deposit insurance schemes' heterogeneity among Member States.

NOTES

1. The sample covers all commercial banks in the euro area on Orbis Bank. Banks that did not report data on net interest income or net fee and commission income from 2017 to 2013 have been excluded from the analysis.
2. Chapter 2 is devoted to analysing NPLs in the euro area banking system.
3. The completion of the Banking Union is addressed in Chaps. 5 and 6.
4. The sample is formed by all euro area commercial banks with data available on Orbis Bank. Since only very few data are available in 2009 and 2010 (for 0 to 12 banks), the analysis is restricted to the 2011–2018 period. Focusing on this period of time allows the progress made since 2011 to be captured, when euro area banks were facing the sovereign debt crisis, which had been even more challenging than the global financial crisis for some euro area countries.
5. At the time of writing only some banks from the sample had published 2018 annual reports.

REFERENCES

Berger, A., and D. Humphrey. 1991. The dominance of inefficiencies over scale and product mix economies in banking. *Journal of Monetary Economics* 28.

———. 1992. The megamergers in banking and the use of cost efficiency as an antitrust defines. *Antitrust Bulletin* 37: 541–600.

Berger, A., G.A. Hanweck, and D.B. Humphrey. 1987. Competitive viability in banking. Scale, scope and product mix economies. *Journal of Monetary Economics* 20 (3): 501–520.

EBA. 2018. 2018 EU-wide stress test results, November.

ECB. 2016. Adapting bank business models: Financial stability implications of greater reliance on fee and commission income. *Financial Stability Review* 2.

———. 2017. *Financial integration in Europe*, May.

———. 2018a. *Financial stability review*, May.

———. 2018b. How can euro area banks reach sustainable profitability in the future? *Financial Stability Review*, November. https://www.ecb.europa.eu/pub/fsr/special/html/ecb.fsrart201811_1.en.html.

———. 2018c. Statistical data warehouse. https://sdw.ecb.europa.eu/browse.do?node=9689369.

———. 2018d. *SSM thematic review on profitability and business models. Report on the outcome of the assessment.* ECB Banking Supervision, September.

———. 2018e. Financial integration in Europe, May.

Goldman Sachs. 2018. Marcus by Goldman Sachs launches in the UK. https://www.goldmansachs.com/media-relations/press-releases/current/marcus-by-goldman-sachs-launches-in-the-uk.html.

IMF. 2018. *Euro area policies: Financial sector assessment program – Technical note – Systemic risk analysis*, July.
Molyneux, P., Y. Altunbas, and E.P.M. Gardener. 1996. *Efficiency in European banking*. John Wiley and Sons.
Philippon, T. 2018. *The FinTech opportunity*. New York University, Stern School of Business, Mimeo.
Reuters. 2018. Goldman Sachs opens digital consumer bank in Britain. https://www.reuters.com/article/us-goldman-sachs-britain/goldman-sachs-opens-digital-consumer-bank-in-britain-idUSKCN1L814J.
Revell, J. 1997. *The recent evolution of financial systems*. St. Martin's Press.
Sironi, A. 2018. *The evolution of banking regulation since the financial crisis: A critical assessment*. Baffi Carefin Centre Research Paper No. 2018-103.

CHAPTER 2

The Main Challenges Facing the Euro Area Banking System

2.1 Introduction

This chapter presents the first of the main issues that are still undermining euro area banking system soundness, that is, the large amount of non-performing loans (NPLs) on banks' balance sheet. The chapter first investigates the European Council "Action plan to address the problem of non-performing loans in the banking sector" and the package of measures presented by the European Commission (EC) in March 2018. For a number of European banks, the main focus of the restructuring work has been on cleaning up their balance sheets by selling off or winding down large non-performing loan portfolios. The new International Financial Reporting Standards (IFRS) accounting standard 9, which makes it less favourable to keep NPLs on the balance sheet, has made it possible to free up internal resources.[1]

This chapter provides insights into changing regulations and introduces the role of the European Central Bank (ECB) in the field of NPL management by banks and the de-risking pattern and speed to be followed, since the ECB has no regulatory powers, but only supervisory powers (embedded in the SREP-II pillar of Basel 3). A comparison of the European Council Action Plan on NPLs presented by the EC in March 2018 with the last addendum of the ECB on the same topic is provided.

The other two main issues underlying euro area banking system fragility, namely the Level 3 assets evaluation and the high exposure of many banks to the debts of their own governments, are investigated in Chap. 4.

© The Author(s) 2019   21
F. Arnaboldi, *Risk and Regulation in Euro Area Banks*, Palgrave
Macmillan Studies in Banking and Financial Institutions,
https://doi.org/10.1007/978-3-030-23429-4_2

2.2   Non-performing Loans: Why the Supervisory Focus?

One of the key areas for reducing risk and enhancing profitability in the euro area banking sector is the further decline of non-performing loans. The financial crisis and subsequent recession led to more widespread inability of borrowers to pay back their loans, as more households and companies faced continuing payment difficulties and even bankruptcy. Not all countries were impacted in the same way, but NPLs piled up, especially in those states experiencing long or deep economic recession.

High NPLs, in terms of both level and ratios, represent an important challenge for various reasons. First, high NPLs reduce bank profitability due to administrative costs and higher funding costs for banks. Provisioning needs may seriously deplete banks' capital base. In addition, they generate less income for a bank than performing loans and may cause losses that reduce the bank's capital.

Second, NPLs represent a risk for the viability of banks, as they can generate negative cross-border spillovers and can affect market perception of the EU banking sector. Since there are large variations within euro area countries, financial fragmentation increases and capital flows within the single market are undermined.

Third, NPLs tie up significant amounts of a bank's resources, both human and financial, locking up capital to back unproductive assets. This reduces the bank's capacity to lend, including to small- and medium-sized firms. In turn, this negative effect in terms of credit supply also reduces the capacity of businesses to invest, thereby creating a tangible effect on the real economy.

In order to reduce the high NPL level and ratios, the European Union agreed on a comprehensive set of measures outlined in the Council of the European Union's "Action Plan to Tackle NPLs in Europe" in 2017, which is currently being implemented. The Council agreed to revert to the issue regularly, and to take stock of the evolution of NPLs in Europe and of actions taken. Before reviewing the various measures adopted at the EU level to tackle NPLs, reduce risk and enhance the resilience of European banking sector in Sect. 2.4, Sect. 2.3 investigates the recent developments in the euro area countries in non-performing loans.

2.3   RECENT DEVELOPMENTS IN NON-PERFORMING LOANS

Non-performing loans are generally defined as bank loans that are subject to late repayment or unlikely to be repaid without requiring the sale of collateral (see, among others, Council of the European Union 2017a). For the purposes of this chapter, the term NPLs refers to non-performing exposures (NPEs) that are over 90 days past due or individually impaired. The financial crisis and subsequent recessions have left banks in some euro area countries with particularly high levels of NPLs. Figure 2.1 reports data on average NPLs by bank for a sample of about 2000 euro area commercial, savings and cooperative institutions.[2]

The average volume of NPLs by bank has continued its steady decline from 2013, decreasing from a bank average of more than 600 million euro to about 400 million euro. In the five-year period under scrutiny, both larger banks—that is, banks with total assets above the sample mean in 2017—and smaller banks experienced a sharp decline in NPLs (−22 and −21 per cent, respectively). This reduction was mainly the result of one-off events that impacted all bank size classes.

Also, the quality of banks' loans portfolios continues to improve. As reported in Fig. 2.2, the NPL-to-gross-loan ratio decreased for all banks

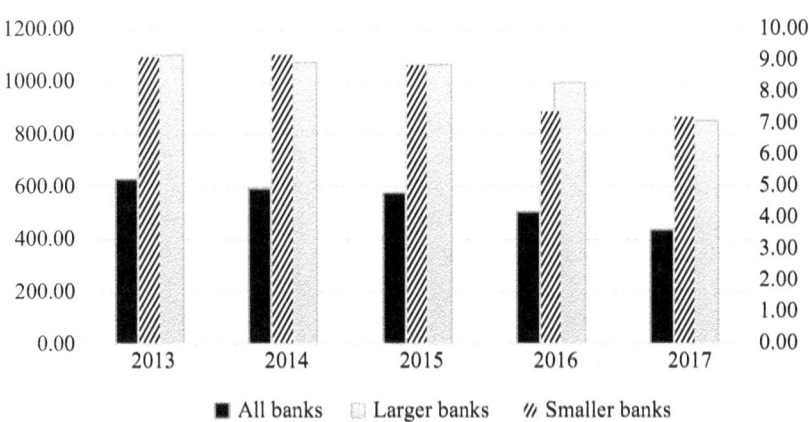

Fig. 2.1   Euro area average NPL by bank (euro mn). Source: Author's elaboration on Orbis Bank data. Note: All banks and larger banks data are reported on the Y left-hand axis, smaller banks data on the Y right-hand axis

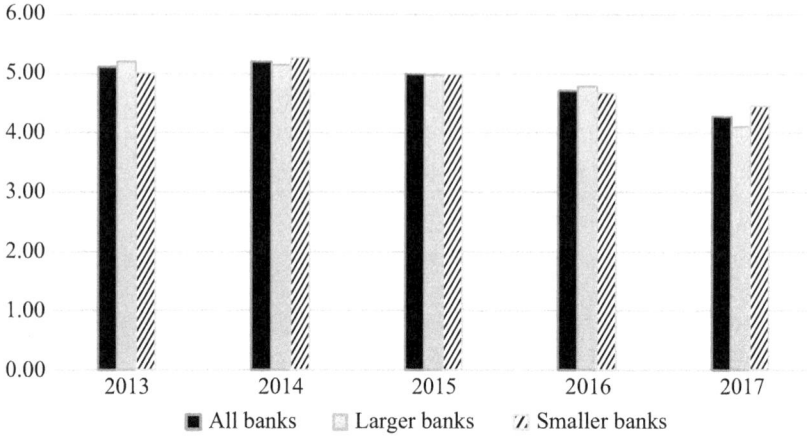

Fig. 2.2 Euro area NPL-to-gross-loans ratio (%). Source: Author's elaboration on Orbis Bank data

from 2013 by 17 per cent on average. This was the result of stabilising economies coupled with various proactive measures, including sales of NPL portfolios. Nevertheless, the slow progress in some euro area countries, as well as the widespread dispersion among countries, remains a concern. The differences between larger and smaller banks' ratios is negligible (4.11 vs. 4.46 per cent in 2017, respectively), but larger banks seem better equipped to reduce the ratio over the five years (−21 per cent compared to −11 per cent, respectively). In sum, larger banks have a similar quality of loan portfolio, measured by the NPLs-to-gross-loans ratio, to smaller banks, but were able to reduce their credit risk more significantly.

In terms of solidity, Fig. 2.3 reports data on the NPLs-to-equity ratio. On average, the ratio of the euro area banks in the sample decreased by 32 per cent. Smaller banks reported a slightly sharper decline than larger banks (−31.6 vs. −29.6 per cent, respectively). The declining trend is, however, different between the two groups. Smaller banks' ratio increased in 2014 from 33 to 38.4 per cent and then decreased stably to 22.6 in 2017. Larger banks' ratio decreased from 45.3 per cent in 2013 to 39.4 per cent in 2015, but then peaked again in 2016 (40.7 per cent). In 2017, it ended at 31.9 per cent. However, despite the ongoing downward trend, the total volume of NPLs remains at an elevated level, especially for smaller banks. Structural impediments continue to hamper banks' efforts to

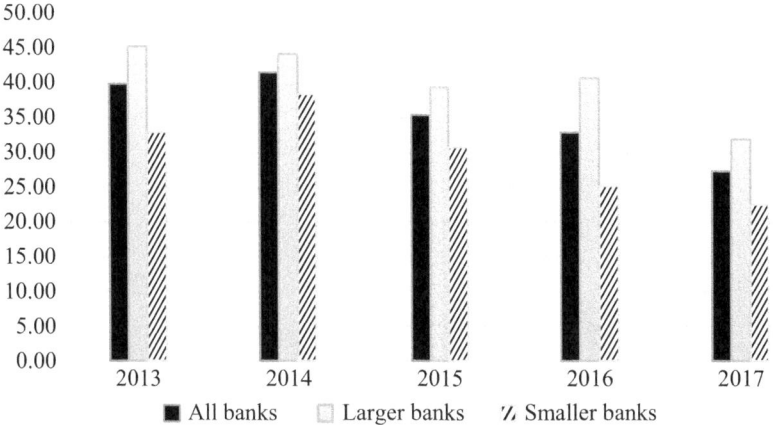

Fig. 2.3 Euro area NPL-to-equity ratio (average %). Source: Author's elaboration on Orbis Bank data

reduce their NPL stocks. Among other elements, activity in secondary markets for NPLs is not yet sufficient to contribute substantially to NPL reduction efforts.

Figure 2.4 shows the NPLs-to-gross-loans ratio by euro area country. Again, the level and trend of the ratio significantly differ among countries. In particular, some countries, such as Germany, Portugal and Estonia, have been able to reduce the ratio in the last five years, whereas some others experienced a rise until 2016.

There are also large variations within the EU when considering the NPLs-to-equity ratio (Fig. 2.5). The average ratio decreased from 94 in 2013 to 60 per cent in 2017, with a standard deviation that also decreased from 82.6 to 63.13. In 2017, the ratio ranged from 8.14 per cent in Estonia to almost 290 per cent in Greece in the sample under scrutiny.

The heterogeneity of NPL levels and ratios within euro area banking systems is confirmed by data in Table 2.1. Both at the beginning and at the end of the sample period, the level of NPLs, the NPLs-to-gross loans ratio and the NPLs-to-equity ratio were significantly higher in Southern than in Northern euro area countries.

As for bank size, clearly the level of NPLs is significantly higher in larger banks, but on average the NPLs-to-gross loans ratio is not significantly different between smaller and larger banks (Table 2.2). Regardless of the size of the bank, NPLs represent a critical issue.

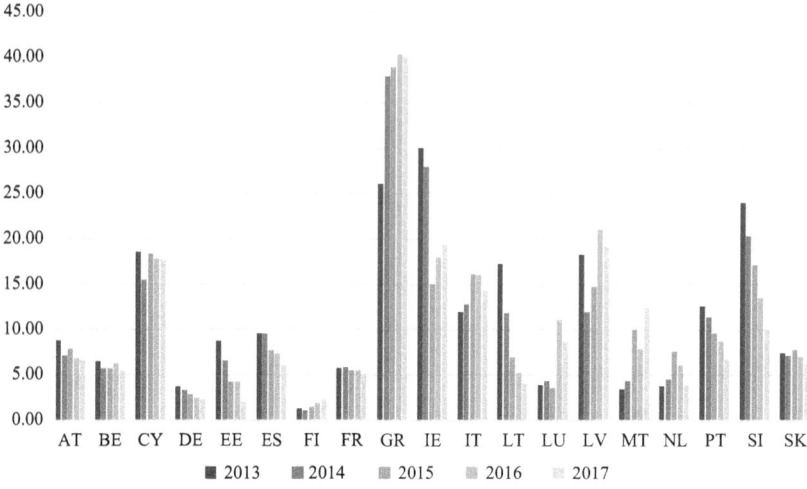

Fig. 2.4 NPL-to-gross-loans ratio by country (%). Source: Author's elaboration on Orbis Bank data

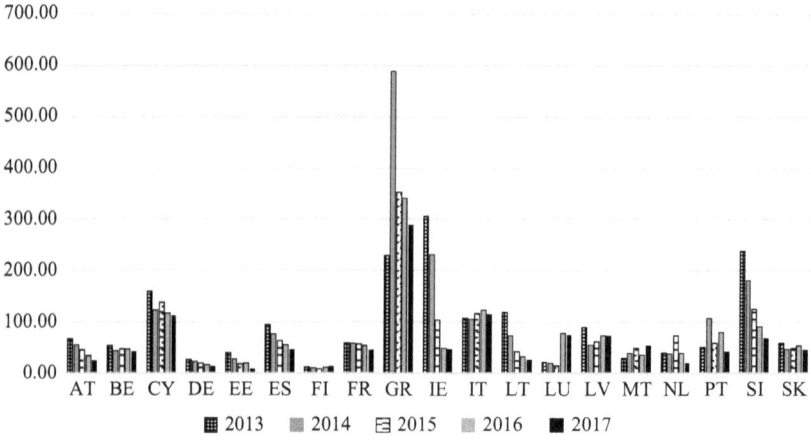

Fig. 2.5 NPL-to-equity ratio by country (%). Source: Author's elaboration on Orbis Bank data

Although banks are primarily responsible for restructuring their business models and resolving their NPL issues, NPLs in some euro area countries may not decline at a sufficient pace, given their current magnitude, despite the economic recovery. The Council of the European Union

Table 2.1 Test for difference in means—NPL level and ratios in Southern and Northern euro area countries

	Southern euro area countries		Northern euro area countries		Difference in means
	No. Obs	Mean	No. Obs	Mean	
Panel A—2013					
NPL (euro mn)	291	2388.96	1212	199.74	2189.22***
NPL to gross loans (%)	291	9.7	1212	4.1	5.6***
NPL to equity (%)	291	86.85	1212	28.2	58.65***
Panel B—2017					
NPL (euro mn)	442	1455.686	1482	127.5431	1328.14***
NPL to gross loans (%)	442	9.04	1477	2.83	6.21***
NPL to equity (%)	442	67.11	1478	15.13	51.98***

Source: Author's elaboration on Orbis Bank data

Note: The table reports the summary statistics (number of observations, mean values and differences in means) for the banks' variables in 2013 and 2017. The t-statistics are calculated using standard errors clustered at the bank level are reported in parentheses. *, ** and *** indicate significance at 10%, 5% and 1% levels, respectively

Table 2.2 Test for difference in means—NPL level and ratios in smaller and larger euro area banks

	Smaller banks		Larger banks		Difference in means
	No. Obs	Mean	No. Obs	Mean	
Panel A—2013					
NPL (euro mn)	658	10.04	845	1101.38	−1091.33***
NPL to gross loans (%)	658	5.1	845	5.2	−0.1
NPL to equity (%)	658	32.16	845	45.3	−13.14***
Panel B—2017					
NPL (euro mn)	959	7.17	965	855.50	−848.34***
NPL to gross loans (%)	958	4.41	961	4.11	0.3
NPL to equity (%)	958	22.3	961	31.89	−9.59***

Source: Author's elaboration on Orbis Bank data

Note: The table reports the summary statistics (number of observations, mean values and differences in means) for the banks' variables in 2013 and 2017. The t-statistics are calculated using standard errors clustered at the bank level are reported in parentheses. *, ** and *** indicate significance at 10%, 5% and 1% levels, respectively

(2017b) agreed that measures to address NPLs would be beneficial for the EU as a whole. While reviewing the recent regulatory steps taken to tackle the issue, the next section also examines incentives for banks to deal with NPLs proactively while avoiding the disruptive effects of fire sales, and measures to address existing stocks of NPLs and prevent further accumulation of NPLs in the future.

2.4   LEGISLATIVE FRAMEWORK TO ADDRESS NPLs

As shown by data presented in the previous section, by 2016 the NPL situation had not resolved itself sufficiently. The NPL issue was not solely the result of the economic crisis but also partly the result of improper credit screening, recognition, inadequate or delayed provisioning and internal governance by banks (EC 2018a). Data show that, while high NPL levels and ratios are not a system-wide problem across the euro area banking system, their persistence in some European countries and the overall size of NPLs in Europe could give rise to financial instability and macroprudential risks and undermine efforts to achieve sustainable growth both in these countries and across the whole EU. Addressing the risks related to high stocks of NPLs is primarily the responsibility of banks and national regulatory authorities. However, the above-mentioned motives explain why the NPL issue came under the European authorities' spotlight. Table 2.3 reports the main actions taken at the EU level to address the NPL issue.

The Subgroup on Non-Performing Loans of the Council's Financial Services Committee (FSC) was established in July 2016 in order to "assess the state of play regarding current NPL stocks and related developments in member states and at EU level, as well as the relevant legal framework at national and EU level" and to deliver "possible options supporting a significant and sustainable reduction of NPL levels, based on the current diverse situations assessed" (Council of the European Union 2017a, p. 3). The Mandate of the Subgroup established by the FSC divided the work into three areas, namely stocktaking, analysis of current policies and establishing policy options and areas for action. The interim report, which was established in December 2016, covered the first two areas, while a final report was presented in May 2017.

The FSC comprehensive report highlights the complexity of the issue and the difficulties in addressing it with a handful of initiatives and policy

Table 2.3 Main EU actions on NPL

Date	EU authority/body	Document
September 2016	ECB	Stocktake of national supervisory practices and legal frameworks related to NPLs
March 2017	ECB	Guidance to banks on non-performing loans
May 2017	Subgroup on Non-Performing Loans of the Council's Financial Services Committee (FSC)	Report of the FSC Subgroup on Non-Performing Loans
June 2017	ECB	Stocktake of national supervisory practices and legal frameworks related to NPLs
July 2017	Council of the European Union	Action plan to tackle non-performing loans in Europe
October 2017	EC	Communication on Completing the Banking Union
January 2018	EC	First Progress Report on the Reduction of Non-Performing Loans in Europe
March 2018	EC	Proposal for a Directive of the European Parliament and of the Council on credit servicers, credit purchasers and the recovery of collateral
March 2018	EC	Proposal for a Regulation of the European Parliament and of the Council on amending Regulation (EU) No. 575/2013 as regards minimum loss coverage for non-performing exposures
March 2018	EC	Blueprint on the set-up of national asset management companies
March 2018	EC	Second Progress Report on the Reduction of Non-Performing Loans in Europe
March 2018	ECB	Addendum to the ECB Guidance to banks on non-performing loans: supervisory expectations for prudential provisioning of non-performing exposures
July 2018	ECB	ECB announces further steps in supervisory approach to stock of NPLs
October 2018	EBA	Guidelines on management of non-performing and forborne exposures
November 2018	EC	Third Progress Report on the Reduction of Non-Performing Loans in Europe
December 2018	EBA	Guidelines on disclosure of non-performing and forborne exposures
January 2019	ESRB	Macroprudential approaches to non-performing loans

Source: Author's elaboration on Council of the European Union (2017a, b), EBA (2018a, b), ECB (2016, 2017a, b, 2018a, b, c), EC (2018a, b, c, d, e) and ESRB (2019)

measures. In fact, important efforts have been undertaken by euro area countries, particularly Ireland, Spain, Italy, Portugal, Greece and Cyprus, to address high NPL levels and ratios (for further details see Council of the European Union 2017a). A number of policy reforms have already been completed, such as the ECB supervisory guidance to banks on non-performing loans (ECB 2017a). The guidance provides recommendations to banks and sets out a number of best practices by addressing the main aspects regarding banks' strategy, governance and operations, which are the key to successfully resolving NPL. Nevertheless, experience shows that reforms aimed at tackling NPLs take time and need to be strengthened before they have a material impact on NPL levels.

On this basis, the Council of the European Union adopted a comprehensive "Action Plan To Tackle Non-Performing Loans in Europe" on 11 July 2017. This plan calls upon various actors to take appropriate measures to further address the challenges of high NPLs, recognising the delicate balance between necessary actions by banks, Member States and the EU. It invites the European Commission, the ECB, the European Banking Authority (EBA), the European Systemic Risk Board (ESRB) and the Member States to take steps on several fronts to tackle both the legacy stock of NPLs and the risk of build-up in the future. In order to achieve this, the Action Plan identifies four main areas where further action is needed: (1) supervision, (2) reform of restructuring, insolvency and debt recovery frameworks, (3) development of secondary markets for distressed assets and (4) fostering restructuring of the banking system (Council of the European Union 2017b). The Council also established a strict monitoring, initially after six months, of the evolution of NPLs in Europe and the development of secondary markets for NPL transactions, to assess the progress made and to guarantee a coordinated approach at EU level.

In line with the Council of the European Union's road map, the EC announced in its "Communication on completing the banking union" of October 2017 a comprehensive package of measures to address the NPL issue. In principle, as requested by the Council, the EC (2017) clarifies the interpretation of Article 16 of Council Regulation (EU) No. 1024/2013 and Article 104 of Directive 2013/36/EU (CRD IV) and confirms that the existing supervisory powers laid down in EU legislation allow the competent authorities to influence a bank's provisioning policy with regard to NPLs. This interpretation sets the ground for the subsequent EC steps. Then the EC (2017) illustrates the main initiatives included in the package, such as measures to further develop secondary markets for NPLs, with the aim of removing impediments to the transfer of loans; measures to enhance the protection of secured creditors; the possible introduction of statutory (Pillar 1) prudential backstops in order to prevent the build-up and potential underprovisioning of future NPLs via time-bound prudential deductions from own funds; a blueprint for how national asset management companies (AMCs) can be set up, managed and closed down within the existing set of banking and state aid rules; and the introduction of a common definition of non-performing exposures (NPEs) in accordance with that already used for supervisory reporting purposes.

Before finalising the package of proposals, the EC overviewed the progress made in implementing the action plan and examined the developments of NPLs in the EU as a whole and within each Member State (EC 2018a). Then, in March 2018, the European Commission presented the announced package, which includes a proposal for a directive on credit servicers, credit purchasers and the recovery of collateral, a proposal for a regulation amending the capital requirements regulation and a blueprint on the set-up of national asset management companies. In addition to the package, the Commission also presented its second progress report on the reduction of NPLs in Europe, which highlighted the further decline of NPL stocks (EC 2018e).

The package sets a road map to further reduce NPLs and reinforce the EU banking system. First, banks are required to put aside sufficient resources when new loans become non-performing. These resources cannot be used for further investments, so they create appropriate incentives for banks to manage NPLs at an early stage and avoid too large an accumulation of NPLs. However, and this is a second step, if loans become non-performing, more efficient enforcement mechanisms for secured loans should allow banks to manage NPLs, subject to appropriate safeguards for debtors and with the exception of loans granted to consumers. Third, if the NPL level is too high, despite the measures mentioned above, the EC establishes rules to allow banks to sell NPLs on efficient, competitive and transparent secondary markets. As a final step, if NPLs have become a significant and broad-based problem, countries can set up national AMCs or other measures under current state aid and bank resolution rules to address the issue (EC 2018e).

2.4.1 Proposal for a Regulation Amending the Capital Requirements Regulation

The Commission launched a consultation in November 2017 to assess whether it was appropriate to introduce a prudential backstop to address underprovisioning for NPLs. The goal was to collect private and public stakeholders' views on the feasibility of a prudential backstop, its possible design and possible unintended consequences. As regards the design of a prudential backstop, most stakeholders were in favour of a progressive path of deduction, as it would better recognise early recoveries of loans. Also, it was argued that a distinction between an NPL where the debtor is still paying its loan and an NPL where the debtor is insolvent should be taken into consideration (EC 2018f).

The proposal for a regulation amending the capital requirements regulation follows both suggestions, while requiring banks to have sufficient loan loss coverage for newly originated loans if these become non-performing exposures (EC 2018c). The proposal introduces a statutory prudential backstop to reduce the risk of underprovisioning of future NPLs. Such a backstop amounts to minimum coverage levels of provisions and deductions from own funds that banks will be required to have for incurred and expected losses on newly originated loans that later become non-performing (EC 2018c). In the case where a bank did not meet the applicable minimum level, deductions from own funds would apply.

Following the Council's action plan, the EC (2018c) also introduced a common definition of non-performing exposures (NPEs), in line with the one already used for supervisory reporting purposes. The prudential backstop has the aim of reducing financial instability arising from high levels of insufficiently covered NPEs, by avoiding their increase and potential spillovers in adverse market conditions. If banks have sufficiently covered losses for NPEs in good times, their profitability, capital and funding costs should be less affected by adverse scenarios. In addition, stable and less pro-cyclical financing could be available to households and firms.

2.4.2 Proposal for a Directive on Credit Servicers, Credit Purchasers and the Recovery of Collateral

In July 2017, the Commission launched a public consultation with a view to exploring possible initiatives to facilitate the development of secondary markets for NPLs. The goal of the consultation was to gather inputs on ways to improve the functioning of the secondary market and more specifically on loan servicing activities by third parties and the transfer of loans away from the originating bank. In this framework, the proposal for a directive on credit servicers, credit purchasers and the recovery of collateral sets the goal of enabling banks to deal in a more efficient way with loans once these become non-performing (EC 2018d). The proposal improves conditions to either enforce the collateral used to secure the credit or to sell the credit to third parties.

On the first topic, the proposal helps banks to better manage NPLs by increasing the efficiency of debt recovery procedures through the availability of a distinct common accelerated extrajudicial collateral enforcement (AECE) procedure. In the majority of cases, banks address their NPLs themselves. A large proportion of the loans that become NPLs are loans secured by collateral. While banks can enforce collateral under national rules, the process can often be slow and unpredictable. In the meantime, NPLs remain on banks' balance sheets, keeping the banks exposed to prolonged uncertainty and reducing resources available for investments. This also prevents the banks from focusing on new lending to viable customers.

Therefore, the proposal makes available more efficient methods for recovering money from secured loans to business borrowers out of court. This extrajudicial procedure would be accessible when agreed upon in advance by both lender and borrower in the loan agreement. It will not be applicable for consumer credits and is designed so as not to affect preventive restructuring or insolvency proceedings and not to change the hierarchy of creditors in insolvency. Because it is easier to price a collateralised NPL than an unsecured one in secondary markets, as the value of the collateral sets a minimum value for an NPL, credit purchasers should prefer NPLs with the AECE feature, giving additional incentives to banks to use this feature at the origination of new loans. In addition, the harmonisation achieved by AECE would foster the development of pan-European NPL investors, and further improve market liquidity (EC 2018d, e).

On the second issue, the proposal encourages the development of secondary markets for NPLs. Under some circumstances, banks may be unable to efficiently manage their NPLs, thereby recovering less value from their loans than would otherwise be possible. This situation may occur, for example, when banks face a large stock of NPLs and do not have the staff or expertise to properly address the NPL issue. If a bank cannot efficiently manage an NPL, a possible solution may be to outsource the servicing of these loans to a specialised credit servicer or to sell the credit agreement to a purchaser that has the necessary risk appetite and expertise to manage it.

For these reasons, the proposal removes impediments to credit servicing by third parties and to the transfer of credits by introducing a common set of rules that third-party credit servicers need to follow in order to work in the EU. This feature would allow the different legislative frameworks for NPLs among EU Member States to be overcome, with the goal of further developing secondary markets for NPLs. The final effect of the proposal is expected to be a reduction of the cost of entry for potential loan purchasers. A higher number of purchasers on the market mean a more competitive market, leading to higher demand and transaction prices.

2.4.3   Blueprint on the Set-Up of National Asset Management Companies

As part of the package, the EC also provides non-binding guidance on how Member States can set up, if they so wish, national asset management companies in full compliance with EU banking and state aid rules (EC 2018b). The AMC Blueprint provides practical guidance for the design and set-up of AMCs in domestic markets, building upon best practices from past experiences in Member States.

AMCs can be private or (partly) publicly supported. If the country acts like any other economic agent, AMCs are not considered as state aid. However, the Blueprint aims to clarify the design for AMCs with a state aid element, as an exceptional solution, to be fully consistent with the EU legal framework, particularly Directive 2014/59/EU (Bank Recovery and Resolution Directive [BRRD]) and Regulation (EU) No. 806/2014 (Single Resolution Mechanism Regulation [SRMR]) and state aid rules. The Blueprint suggests a number of common principles, such as the relevant asset perimeter, the participation perimeter, considerations on the asset-size threshold, asset valuation rules, the appropriate capital structure and the governance and operations of the AMC. In addition, the Blueprint describes certain alternative impaired asset relief measures that do not constitute state aid, such as market-conform state guarantees enabling the securitisation of NPLs.

2.5   Supervisory Framework on Npls

Addressing the risks related to high stocks of NPLs is important for the economy as a whole, as NPLs weigh on banks' profitability and absorb valuable resources, restricting their ability to grant new loans. Problems in the banking sector can quickly spread to other parts of the economy. Also, the supervisory authority investigated the issue by creating a dedicated NPL task force in 2015.

In September 2016, the European Central Bank published its first stocktake on national supervisory practices and legal frameworks related to NPLs, followed by an update one year later (ECB 2016, 2017b). The ECB goal was to generally promote further dialogue among the parties to finding sustainable solutions to the elevated levels of NPLs within the EU. The first stocktake was completed in collaboration with eight National Competent Authorities (NCAs) focusing in particular on the emerging best practices in jurisdictions with relatively high levels of NPLs. Then the stocktake was extended to the remaining 11 countries participating in the Single Supervisory Mechanism (SSM) so that ECB Banking Supervision would have a full picture of the practices in the euro area as at 31 December 2016. Given that the new countries in the second stocktake do not have high levels of NPLs, the policies and practices in their jurisdictions are not as prescriptive as those in jurisdictions currently reacting to high levels of NPLs (ECB 2017b).

Over time, ECB Banking Supervision has developed a supervisory framework for NPLs. This includes three strategic elements, which either directly address legacy NPLs or aim to prevent the build-up of new NPLs in the future: (1) NPL guidance for significant banks, outlining qualitative supervisory expectations with regard to managing and reducing NPLs; (2) a framework to address NPL stocks as part of the supervisory dialogue, comprising: (a) an assessment of the banks' own NPL reduction strategies and (b) bank-specific supervisory expectations with a view to ensuring adequate provisioning of legacy NPLs; and (3) an addendum to the NPL guidance, outlining quantitative supervisory expectations to foster timely provisioning practices for new NPLs.

The ECB (2017a) guidance follows the life cycle of NPL management. The document starts with the supervisory expectations regarding NPL strategies, which are closely linked to NPL governance and operations. Following this, the guidance outlines important aspects for forbearance treatments and NPL recognition. The document concludes with qualitative guidance on NPL provisioning and write-off and collateral valuations. More specifically, the guidance requires banks to implement ambitious, yet credible portfolio-level reduction strategies, for tackling the NPL stock. These strategies are banks' own plans to reduce non-performing exposures and foreclosed assets and are scrutinised by the joint supervisory teams, through an iterative process between the banks and the teams. The process is integrated into the Supervisory Review and Evaluation Process (SREP).

The supervisory assessment also includes benchmarking analysis in order to ensure a level playing field and sufficiently ambitious and realistic targets. On this note, "ambition" is based on the volumes of reduction as opposed to the absolute NPL ratio, which can be subject to arbitrage depending on the calibration. This approach takes the bank specifics into consideration by accounting for varying bank starting points. The level of ambition is based on the level of gross and net non-performing asset reduction instead of solely NPE reduction to minimise arbitrage. The reduction is measured over a three-year strategy horizon to account for the fact that the NPL reductions option can take time to implement. Furthermore, the ECB on-site inspections of NPL data integrity revealed a lack of risk data aggregation processes for data relevant to the detection of financial difficulties, such as data from income statements, or EBITDA (earnings before interest, tax, depreciation and amortization). It also emerged that the relevant parameters, such as collateral haircuts, discount times and cure rates, are often significantly misestimated and the criteria for write-offs are in many cases not clearly defined (ECB 2018a, b).

In March 2018, the ECB published an addendum to the NPL guidance to further specify the ECB's expectations (ECB 2018a). The addendum distinguishes between secured and unsecured non-performing exposures, where NPEs are considered fully secured if they benefit from credit risk protection that exceeds the current drawn and potential undrawn credit facilities of the debtor. If they do not benefit from credit risk protection, NPEs are considered fully unsecured. A blended approach is applied to NPEs that are partially collateralised, that is, the value of credit risk protection does not exceed the current drawn and potential undrawn credit facilities. Once the bank has established the value of its credit risk protection, the exposure is split in two: (1) secured balance—the bank values the credit risk protection as for fully secured exposures and (2) unsecured balance—the unsecured balance is equal to the original drawn and potential undrawn credit facilities minus the secured balance of the exposure. The ECB has different expectations regarding secured versus unsecured exposures, as summarised in Fig. 2.6.

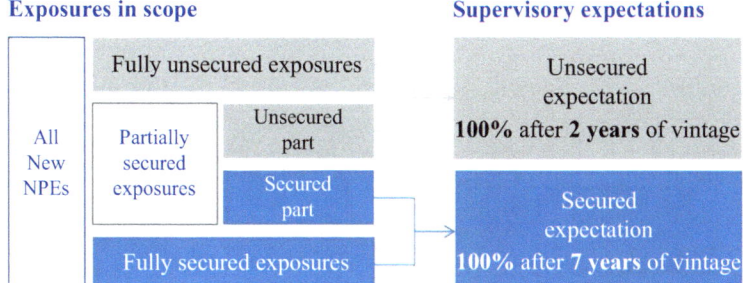

Fig. 2.6 Blended approach for new NPEs in scope. Source: ECB (2018a, p. 8)

For fully unsecured exposures and unsecured parts of partially secured exposures, it is expected that 100 per cent coverage will be achieved within two years of the NPL classification. For fully secured exposures and secured parts of partially secured exposures, it is expected that 100 per cent coverage will be achieved within seven years of the NPL classification, following a gradual path. The different expectations have the aim of avoiding cliff edge effects, and take into consideration the prudential principle that credit risk protection must be enforceable in a timely manner.

The dialogue continues, as the ECB further engaged with each bank to define its supervisory expectations (ECB 2018b). The bank-specific supervisory expectations are based on a benchmarking of comparable banks and guided by individual banks' current NPL ratio and main financial features. The aim is to ensure continued progress to reduce legacy risks in the euro area and achieve the same coverage of the levels and flows of NPLs over the medium term.

On top of this, the ECB is going to take steps to improve the underwriting standards for new loans. Lending practices, both with regard to the quality of credit risk modelling and the stringency of banks' lending appetites, will undergo a review in order to reduce the potential risk. This may also be conducted bank-specifically. This will further be reinforced with on-site inspections, not only in banks but also in other commercial real estate, residential real estate and leverage finance institutions.

2.5.1   European Banking Authority and European Systemic Risk Board

In addition, ECB Banking Supervision supported the European Banking Authority (EBA) in issuing general guidelines on the management of non-performing and forborne exposures, and guidelines on the disclosure of non-performing and forborne exposures (EBA 2018a, b). These guidelines are to be applied by all credit institutions across the EU. With regard to less significant institutions, they are to apply the guidelines in a proportionate manner, as set out in the guidelines.

The EBA (2018a) aims primarily to reduce the number of NPEs on banks' balance sheets by providing supervisory guidance to ensure that banks effectively manage NPEs and forborne exposures (FBEs) on their balance sheets. The aim is to achieve a sustainable reduction of NPEs by means of their own NPE strategies. The guidelines first introduce the requirements of the NPE strategy, providing details on the strategy and outlining the supporting governance and operational arrangements. Then, the document sets out supervisory expectations regarding the use of forbearance, addresses the recognition of NPEs, deals with NPE impairments and write-offs and specifies supervisory requirements regarding the collateral valuation of movable and immovable property. Furthermore, it provides guidance to the competent authorities on addressing NPEs and FBEs in the SREP. The core building block of the guidelines is, however, the strategy for the banks' NPE management. The strategy sets the basis for the banks' initial and regular assessments of the operating environment and describes the considerations that they should take into account. These include the internal capabilities of the credit institution, external conditions and capital implications. When developing their NPE strategy, banks should also consider all available strategic options and combinations of them. These include hold/forbearance strategies, active portfolio reductions, taking collateral onto the balance sheet and legal options including out-of-court options. Furthermore, implementing the operational plan and embedding the NPE strategy into the institution are both important aspects of the NPE strategy. The guidelines call for a regular review of the strategy, monitoring of its operational effectiveness and integration of it into the credit institution's risk management framework.

A second document issued by the EBA is the guidelines on disclosure of non-performing and forborne exposures (EBA 2018b). The guidelines specify the common content and uniform disclosure formats for the information on NPEs, forborne exposures and foreclosed assets that banks should release with the aim of providing meaningful information to market participants on banks' asset quality and of gaining a better insight into the distribution and level of collateralisation of NPEs among banks with a gross NPL ratio of 5 per cent or above, and thus a better understanding of the banks' risk profiles.

The EBA also participated in the European Systemic Risk Board (ESRB) working group that produced the report on macroprudential approaches to non-performing loans, which focuses on the role macroprudential policy can play in preventing system-wide increases in NPLs (ESRB 2019). The report presents the ESRB response to the Council of the European Union request to develop macroprudential approaches to prevent the emergence of system-wide NPL problems (Council of the European Union 2017b). The report starts by identifying the main triggers, vulnerabilities and amplifiers that can drive system-wide increases in NPLs. The drivers include the business cycle and asset price shocks; high indebtedness and excessive credit growth; inadequate bank practices and governance (including loan origination, loan monitoring and NPL early intervention); and a number of structural factors such as the legal and judicial framework. With these drivers in mind, the report then focuses on the role that macroprudential policy can play in preventing system-wide increases in NPLs and in increasing banks' resilience in the face of such increases. No fundamental change to the existing macroprudential toolkits seems to be required, although some refinements should be considered. Nevertheless, further work is needed in areas relating to the use of sectoral capital buffers and the development of borrower-based measures (which are not harmonised at the European level).

2.6   Conclusion

Despite a significant improvement in asset quality in recent years, high levels of NPLs remain a concern for a relevant number of euro area banks. The ongoing implementation of NPL reduction strategies, despite the progress made in reducing the number of legacy NPLs, is still proceeding at a slow pace. The current aggregate level of NPLs remains high, and banks' search for profits could increase the potential for a future build-up of NPLs. European authorities have elaborated a strategy to ensure that the issue of NPLs in the euro area is adequately addressed in such a complex system. This strategy, however, will take time to bear fruit. The next chapter investigates further the NPL issue in the euro area, focusing on the euro area cross-country heterogeneity in the NPL restructuring process.

NOTES

1. It is important to highlight that, in parallel with the supervisory framework discussed in this book, IFRS 9 represented a significant accounting innovation affecting the banking industry. Indeed, even if not directly imposed by the banking regulators, this accounting standard is one of the G20 commitments agreed on directly after the financial crisis to promote a safer and more stable financial system (Sironi 2018).
2. The sample covers all commercial, savings and cooperative banks in the euro area on Orbis Bank. Banks that did not report data on non-performing loans in 2017 have been excluded from the analysis. The sample period started in 2013 due to the scarcity of data available before that year.

REFERENCES

Council of the European Union. 2017a. *Report of the FSC subgroup on non-performing loans*. 9854/17, Brussels, May.
———. 2017b. *Action plan to tackle non-performing loans in Europe*, July.
EBA. 2018a. *Guidelines on management of non-performing and forborne exposures*. EBA/GL/2018/06, October 31.
———. 2018b. *Guidelines on disclosure of non-performing and forborne exposures*. EBA/GL/2018/10, December 17.
EC. 2017. *Communication to the European Parliament, the Council, the European Central Bank, the European Economic and Social Committee and the Committee of the Regions on Completing the Banking Union*. COM (2017) 592 final, October.
———. 2018a. *Commission staff working document, accompanying the document communication from the Commission to the European parliament, the Council and the European Central Bank*. First Progress Report on the Reduction of Non-Performing Loans in Europe COM(2018) 37 final.
———. 2018b. *AMC blueprint accompanying the document communication from the Commission to the European Parliament, the Council and the European Central Bank*. Second Progress Report on the Reduction of Non-Performing Loans in Europe COM(2018) 133 final, SWD(2018) 72 final.
———. 2018c. *Proposal for a Regulation of the European Parliament and of the Council on amending Regulation (EU) No 575/2013 as regards minimum loss coverage for non performing exposures*. COM(2018) 134 final.
———. 2018d. *Proposal for a Directive of the European Parliament and of the Council on credit servicers, credit purchasers and the recovery of collateral*. COM(2018) 135 final.

————. 2018e. *Commission staff working document, Accompanying the document Communication from the Commission to the European Parliament, the Council and the European Central Bank*. Second Progress Report on the Reduction of Non-Performing Loans in Europe COM(2018) 133 final, SWD.(2018) 72 final.

————. 2018f. *Executive summary of the impact assessment, Accompanying the document Proposal for a Regulation of the European Parliament and of the Council amending Regulation (EU) No 575/2013 as regards minimum loss coverage for nonperforming exposures*. SWD(2018) 74 final.

ECB. 2016. *Stocktake of national supervisory practices and legal frameworks related to NPLs*, September.

————. 2017a. *Guidance to banks on non-performing loans*, March.

————. 2017b. *Stocktake of national supervisory practices and legal frameworks related to NPLs*, June.

————. 2018a. *Addendum to the ECB guidance to banks on nonperforming loans: Supervisory expectations for prudential provisioning of non-performing exposures*, March.

————. 2018b. ECB *announces further steps in supervisory approach to stock of NPLs*. Press release, July 11.

————. 2018c. *ECB annual report on supervisory activities 2017*, March.

ESRB. 2019. Macroprudential approaches to non-performing loans, January.

Sironi, A. 2018. *The evolution of banking regulation since the financial crisis: A critical assessment*. Baffi Carefin Centre Research Paper No. 2018-103.

CHAPTER 3

Non-performing Loans in the Euro Area

3.1 Introduction

Since the progress that banks have made in restructuring has varied among countries—depending on the nature of the crisis in their domestic markets, the type of underlying collateral and the strength of creditors' rights—this chapter investigates cross-country heterogeneity in the non-performing loan (NPL) restructuring process focusing on those countries with the highest NPL ratios. NPLs created by local real estate bubbles have proven easier to deal with than NPLs from corporates or small- and medium-sized enterprises (SMEs) in economies struggling for competitiveness. Restructuring loans for corporates and SMEs is typically more difficult as these counterparties are often financed by multiple banks, and creditor coordination therefore becomes more complex. Banks in countries with high NPL ratios are expected to continue the process of restructuring, writing off and selling off NPLs in the next few years to significantly reduce their risk exposure.

3.2 Restructuring Process in High NPL Euro Area Countries

As described in the previous chapter, the decline in NPLs has accelerated over the past two years and has been particularly fast in countries with high NPL ratios (EC 2018). The clean-up of balance sheets will take more

© The Author(s) 2019   43
F. Arnaboldi, *Risk and Regulation in Euro Area Banks*, Palgrave Macmillan Studies in Banking and Financial Institutions,
https://doi.org/10.1007/978-3-030-23429-4_3

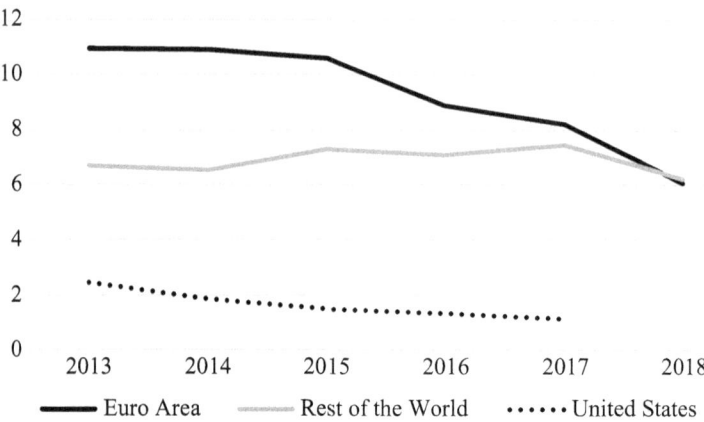

Fig. 3.1 NPL-to-total gross loans ratio average (in percentage). Source: IMF Financial Soundness Indicator (2018a)

time; nevertheless, the aggregate level of NPLs in the euro area banking sector can now be compared to international standards (Fig. 3.1).

Across the euro area, NPL ratios continue to differ significantly from country to country, as shown in Table 3.1. Greek, Cypriot and Portuguese significant banks (SI) have the highest NPL ratios (with country-weighted averages standing at 43.4, 20.7 and 14.5 per cent, respectively, in the third quarter of 2018). Looking at the trend, the NPL ratio decreased significantly year on year for banks in Cyprus (−13.3 percentage points), Slovenia (−5.3 percentage points), Ireland (−3.7 percentage points), Portugal (−3.6 percentage points), Greece (−3.2 percentage points) and Italy (−2.5 percentage points). In the third quarter of 2018, the stock of NPLs was largest in the case of Italian banks (153 billion euro), followed by French (130 billion euro), Spanish (95 billion euro) and Greek institutions (90 billion euro).

This fragmentation is reflected in the different approaches taken at country level to address the NPL issue, which are now investigated for those countries with high NPL levels according to the ECB (2017), that is, Greece, Cyprus, Portugal and Italy. Reducing NPL requires a comprehensive strategy, with initiatives in different areas and coordination between the various stakeholders.

Table 3.1 NPL and advances—amounts and ratios by country (reference period: third quarter of 2018)

Country	Loans and advances (1) (€ bn)	NPL and advances (€ bn)	NPL ratio (percentages)	Year-on-year change in NPL stock (€ bn)	Year-on-year change in NPL ratio (percentage points)
Belgium	493.2	10.4	2.1	−3.1	−0.8
Germany	2811.90	44.3	1.6	−10.9	−0.4
Estonia	C	C	C	C	C
Ireland	243.4	20.6	8.5	−9.2	−3.7
Greece	207.7	90	43.4	−16.3	−3.2
Spain	2349.80	95.4	4.1	−16.5	−0.7
France	4532.80	130.2	2.9	−7.6	−0.3
Italy	1639.80	153.4	9.4	−42.6	−2.5
Cyprus	35.9	7.4	20.7	−10.3	−13.3
Latvia	C	C	C	C	C
Lithuania (2)	29.8	1	3.2	0.4	0.1
Luxembourg	96	1	1	−0.1	−0.4
Malta	14.4	0.5	3.5	0	−0.2
Netherlands	1896.20	36.6	1.9	−3.5	−0.3
Austria	391.2	12.3	3.1	−4.3	−1
Portugal	149.2	21.7	14.5	−5.5	−3.6
Slovenia	15.2	1.3	8.3	−0.8	−5.3
Slovakia (3)	–	–	–	–	–
Finland	C	C	C	C	C
Total	15,058.10	627.7	4.2	−131.4	−1

Source: ECB (2018)

Notes: SI at the highest level of consolidation for which common reporting (COREP) and financial reporting (FINREP) are available. C denotes that the value is not included for confidentiality reasons. (1) Loans and advances in the asset quality tables are displayed at gross carrying amount. In line with FINREP: (a) held for trading exposures are excluded, and (b) cash balances at central banks and other demand deposits are included. (2) The increase in the NPL ratio in LT was driven by a change in the approach to consolidation regarding one SI. (3) There are no SI at the highest level of consolidation in Slovakia

3.2.1   Greece

Figure 3.2 shows the trend of gross loans and gross NPLs in Greece from 2011 to 2018 on a quarterly basis. Though it is not possible to relate these data to the implementation of each reform and regulatory change in the NPL topic, which is described in this section, overall, Fig. 3.2 exhibits an increasing trend in gross NPLs from 2011 up to 2016 (+153 per cent). From the second quarter of 2016 to the end of 2018, the gross NPL amount decreased by 24 per cent, whereas gross loans diminished by 17 per cent.

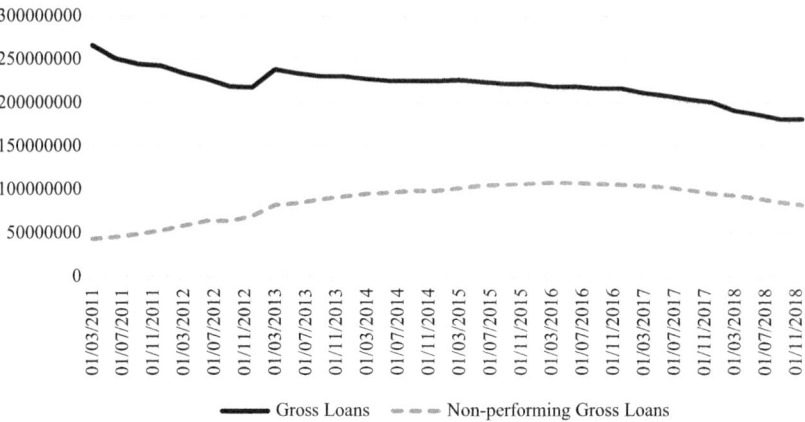

Fig. 3.2   Loans and NPL in Greece (euro thousand). Source: Author's elaboration on Bank of Greece (2019)

3.2.1.1   Regulatory Changes

In May 2014, the Bank of Greece adopted an Executive Committee Act (42/30 May 2014) laying down a specific framework of requirements for the management of exposures in arrears and non-performing loans by banks. This framework imposes obligations on banks, that is, to establish an independent arrears and NPL management (ANPLM) function, to develop a separate, documented ANPLM strategy, the implementation of which is supported by appropriate management information systems and procedures, and to report to the management of the banks and the Bank of Greece on a regular basis. The ANPLM function should include portfolio segmentation to enable banks to choose and tailor different management solutions in different segments of their loan books (Bank of Greece 2014).

About one year later, in February 2015, the Executive Committee Act 47/9 introduced modifications and improvements to reporting templates under the 2014 Executive Committee Act, such as a detailed segmentation of portfolios in accordance with the general principle of "mutually exclusive" segments, information by portfolio segment and arrears bucket, the establishment of a new subcategory of denounced exposures under non-performing exposures (NPEs), due to the need to monitor these exposures separately, a detailed account of legal workout activities, the breakdown of collateral by type of collateral and a sectoral breakdown of corporate loans and minimum standardisation and classification of widely applied forbearance measures and resolution and closure solutions in 22 indicative types (Bank of Greece 2015).

In 2016, following consultation with public entities, supervised institutions and consumer organisations, the Bank of Greece introduced a revised Code of Conduct on Loans in Arrears (the Code of Conduct) by Decision 195/1/29.07.2016 of the Credit and Insurance Committee of the Bank of Greece. The Code intended to standardise the policies and procedures to be applied by the banks for the purposes of identifying and implementing forbearance, resolution and closure solutions for loans in arrears by reference to specific categories of borrowers. The revised Code of Conduct is binding on banks as well as servicing companies and companies having acquired bank loan and credit receivables. The Code provides that its procedures apply in respect of debtors being individuals, professionals and small businesses with an average turnover of less than 1 million euro during the last three years and distinguishes between cooperating and non-cooperating borrowers. Furthermore, it introduces the notion of reasonable living expenses and requires specific policies for debtors belonging to socially vulnerable groups. It also requires the assessment of recovery solutions by reference to the net present value of settlement plans and a recent estimate of the liquidation value, where a forbearance solution has been ruled out and a resolution and closure action is proposed instead. Then the Bank of Greece further modified the reporting templates to include (1) data for monitoring the operational targets and Key Performance Indicators (KPIs) on NPLs and the actions to manage loans in arrears in accordance with the revised Code of Conduct, and (2) auction procedure, collateral obtained by taking possession and participation to out-of-court procedures (Bank of Greece 2016, 2018a, b).

3.2.1.2 Centralised Management Scheme

Despite all these measures, the NPL ratio remains high, primarily due to the absence of credit expansion as well as deleveraging of bank balance sheets (Bank of Greece 2018c). Therefore, at the end of 2018, to systemically address the NPL issue, the Bank of Greece proposed creating a centralised management scheme to transfer a significant part of non-performing exposures (NPEs) along with part of the deferred tax credits (DTCs), which are booked on bank balance sheets, to a Special Purpose Vehicle (SPV). As illustrated by the Bank of Greece (2018c), to finance the transfer, the SPV proceeds with a securitisation issue, comprising (indicatively) three classes of notes (senior, mezzanine, subordinated junior/equity). The lower class of notes (subordinated junior/equity) should be subscribed to by banks (each participating by no more than 20 per cent) and the Greek state. The scheme will be managed exclusively by private investors (servicing companies for loans and credits), and apparently there will be an asset class separation for each transaction and management operation (business, mortgage, consumer loans, etc.). The rapid resolution of the NPL issue has been recognised as a relevant matter for restarting the Greek economy and restoring significant and sustainable growth rates, especially because bank lending is the predominant source of corporate and household finance. It is obvious that a move like the one described above would bring a direct and drastic reduction in the ratio of non-performing exposures and would allow, under certain conditions, the targeting of a single-digit NPL ratio by 2022. Moreover, it would establish favourable conditions for supporting operating profitability and internal capital generation because of improved asset quality and resilience to shocks in any future crisis. Finally, it would enable the business model of banks to be reshaped and the uncertainty regarding their medium-term prospects alleviated.

3.2.1.3   *Asset Protection Scheme*
A second proposal is the asset protection scheme (APS), which was suggested by the Greek finance ministry and by the bank rescue fund the Hellenic Financial Stability Fund (HFSF). The HFSF fund holds significant stakes in the National Bank of Greece, Piraeus Bank, Eurobank and Alpha Bank after taking part in their recapitalisations. The APS scheme involves an SPV that would issue bonds with a government guarantee for senior tranches, similarly to Italy's state guarantee model (GACS), which will be illustrated in Sect. 3.2.4. At the time of writing, the government had submitted the APS plan to the European Union authorities. The APS scheme could need state guarantees of 5 to 7 billion euro, to be used only if needed. About 15 billion euro of bad loans could be securitised via the APS model, according to HFSF CEO Martin Czurda. That would reduce the NPL ratio close to European averages. In the Bank of Greece model, up to 40 billion euro could be shifted to an SPV (Georgiopoulos and Papadimas 2019).

3.2.2   *Cyprus*
Figure 3.3 exhibits details on loans and advances in Cyprus in 2014 and 2017 (EBA 2015, 2018). The gross NPL amount decreased by 56 per cent in three years; also, the collaterals and guarantees received on NPEs diminished by 69 per cent in the same time span.

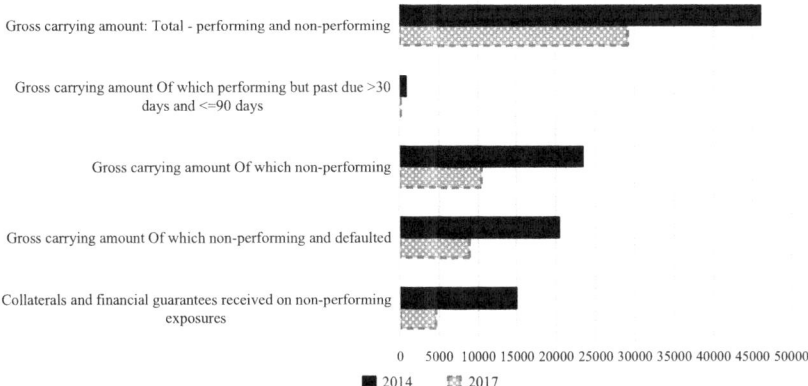

Fig. 3.3 Loans and advances in Cyprus (euro million). Source: Author's elaboration on EBA (2015, 2018) available at: https://eba.europa.eu/risk-analysis-and-data/eu-wide-transparency-exercise/2018

3.2.2.1 Regulatory Changes

In this framework, several legislative and regulatory changes have been introduced in the country and are now illustrated. Although it is not possible to measure the impact of each reform on the stock of NPLs, the overall effect goes in the direction of reducing the non-performing exposure of Cypriot banks, reflecting mainly write-offs and the sale of loans, and supported by a strong economic recovery. This declining effect is, however, due to the most recent reforms. Indeed, early legislative reforms failed to address the large stock of NPLs. This failure partly reflects weaknesses in the legal framework and a lack of enforcement (IMF 2018b).

Before the global financial crisis, the legal and institutional systems in Cyprus appeared to adequately support the growing economy. Cyprus is a mixed-law system with a strong common-law influence. Much of the legislation is still based on mid-last century English law, while selected areas reflect influences from other systems and, following accession to the EU, the law of the European Union (IMF 2017). However, the crisis exposed the underlying weaknesses: for example, procedures for the issuance of title deeds for real estate had not kept up with the real estate boom of the early-mid 2000s, and delays in court proceedings were on the rise. In particular, it became apparent that the existing laws and procedures for debt enforcement and debt restructuring were inadequate: the enforcement regime was weak and slow, foreclosure took years and insolvency laws were outdated. Substantial delays in processing cases through the courts made the resolution of commercial disputes lengthy and inefficient (IMF 2017). Early actions to deal with NPLs focused on promoting voluntary negotiations.

In 2013, the Central Bank of Cyprus (CBC) adopted the Directive on Arrears Management, which included a Code of Conduct for banks.[1] The Directive required banks to offer troubled borrowers customised restructuring solutions and provided banks with guidance on engaging with borrowers and multi-creditor coordination. Consideration was also given to expanding the role of the Financial Ombudsman in facilitating negotiations between debtors and creditors. At the same time, the authorities undertook a review of the corporate and household debt restructuring framework to identify impediments to debt restructuring and measures to address them.

Given the magnitude of the gaps, and the variety of topics under discussion, the authorities decided to tackle them through a comprehensive reform strategy adopted by the Council of Ministers in July 2014, whose goal was to strengthen the foreclosure regime, to reform the corporate and personal insolvency regime and to support the new insolvency framework.[2]

The Council of Ministers adopted widely tested solutions: for instance, the new insolvency regime was modelled on that of Ireland. The reforms were designed to balance the interests of creditors and debtors and were carefully coordinated but still proved difficult.

Even after the reform, the use of the foreclosure framework was limited because it was uncertain whether the new procedure applied for legacy cases, foreclosure auctions remained unpopular and often faced protests, and potential court delays due to challenges and appeals discouraged the use of the new procedure. Personal repayment plans (PRPs), introduced in the 2015 reform of insolvency framework, have also rarely been used. Furthermore, until recently, the sale of NPL portfolios has been limited. Changes to accounting rules, which allow banks to take extra provisions on bad loans without having to raise fresh capital, have provided new stimulus to lenders to sell NPLs. For instance, in 2018, the Bank of Cyprus sold a portfolio of loans to companies and small businesses secured against property with a gross book value of 2.8 billion euro, of which 2.7 billion euro are classified as non-performing (Rutter Pooley and Smith 2018). Apollo Global, a US-based private equity firm, financed the deal through a securitisation structure, following the approval of the law on securitisation of bad loans (Law Providing for the Securitisation of Credit Facilities or Other Exposures and for Related Issues—The Securitisation Law of 2018). The securitisation law aimed to make foreclosure a more credible threat to debtors and to make the insolvency framework more usable. The 2018 amendments also clarified that the law applies to legacy cases, allowed the introduction of electronic auctions and further facilitated the auction process. The Bank of Cyprus deal's structure follows the usual pattern with senior debt raised against the portfolio, equivalent to at least 65 per cent of the purchase price. The Bank of Cyprus provided 450 million euro of this senior financing, while Apollo Global invested in a junior tranche that ranks behind it.

3.2.2.2 ESTIA Scheme

More ambitious reforms were passed in 2018 (IMF 2018b). The amendments addressed some of the shortcomings of previous reforms. For example, the amendments to the Immovable Property (Transfer and Mortgage) Law allow creditors to break down a mortgage into multiple pieces and to give loan buyers increased access to data to assess debtors' indebtedness. Increased information availability may help in finding a tentative agreement on a sale of loans of a significant amount.

Partly due to the limited use of foreclosure and insolvency tools so far, the preferred modalities for NPL resolution have been write-offs and the sale of loans. From mid-2017 to June 2018, outflows from NPLs were almost three times the inflows to NPLs. The outflows from NPLs consisted of write-offs (about one-third), sale of loans (one-third), migration to performing category (20 per cent), NPL cash repayment (10 per cent) and debt to asset or equity swaps (6 per cent) (IMF 2018b). With further sale of loans, NPLs are expected to decline on bank balance sheets. Furthermore, the bulk of the NPLs previously owned by the Cyprus Cooperative Bank (CCB) were moved out of the banking sector in the third quarter of 2018 to a newly created state-owned asset management company.

Outflows from NPLs by cash repayments or migration into the performing category have not substantially accelerated despite a strong economic recovery. Even with GDP growth above 4 per cent annually since 2016 and a strong recovery in employment, the size of cash repayments or migration into the performing category has not substantially increased, implying that the payment discipline remains weak. However, inflows into NPLs are on a declining trend, likely reflecting stricter lending standards (IMF 2018b).

Cypriot banks face declining interest margins like all other EU banks and this puts pressure on profits. On top of that, they also need to accumulate provisions, as continued difficulties in collateral recovery have increased the risk that the transaction price of NPLs may be lower than their book value, leading banks to further recognise losses. More recently, however, the accumulation of provisions has facilitated the sale of NPLs by banks. To further address the NPL issue, in March 2019, the government launched ESTIA, a one-off scheme with the goal of achieving a socially acceptable solution to the problem of debt-overburdened households, while at the same time contributing to the deleverage of Cypriot banks. According to the terms of the scheme, the income threshold for participating ranges from 20,000 euro for single applicants to 60,000 euro per annum for couples with four or more dependent members, and the primary residence that is mortgaged must have a maximum market value of up to 350,000 euro. The loans have to be written down to the market value of the primary residence and then the borrower has to pay two-thirds of the rescheduled loan every month. One-third of the restructured loan instalments is subsidised by the state. The scheme applies to mortgages that were classified as non-performing as on 30 September 2017. Loans designated as non-performing after that date are not eligible (Andreou and Koutsampelas 2019).

3.2.3   Portugal

Similar to Greece and Cyprus, Fig. 3.4 shows the gross carrying amount of loans and advances in Portugal in 2014 and 2017, which increased by 15 per cent. In the same period, the gross NPL amount increased by 14 per cent.

3.2.3.1 Regulatory Changes: The First Pillar
The quality of loan portfolios of Portuguese banks seems not to have improved significantly despite the regulatory and legislative changes that have been passed. In this country, the strategy for reducing NPLs is based primarily on three interdependent and complementary pillars: (1) revision of the legal, judicial and fiscal framework; (2) microprudential supervisory actions, under the SSM; and (3) management of the NPL portfolios, including possible systemic measures.

In terms of the first pillar, legislative amendments have been introduced to correct some of the inadequacies of the framework previously in

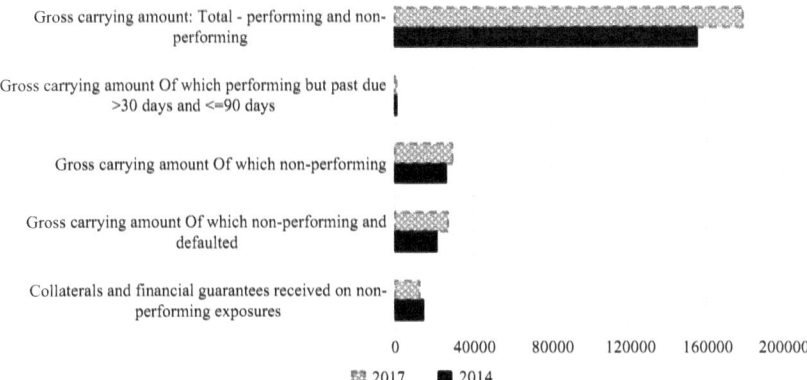

Fig. 3.4 Loans and advances in Portugal (euro million). Source: Author's elaboration on EBA (2015, 2018) available at: https://eba.europa.eu/risk-analysis-and-data/eu-wide-transparency-exercise/2018

force. Through the Resolution of the Council of Ministers No. 42/2016, of 18 August 2016, and based on the work of Estrutura de Missão para a Capitalização de Empresas ("Mission Structure for the Capitalization of Companies"), the government approved the Programa Capitalizar ("Programme to Capitalize"), a strategic initiative to support the capitalisation of firms, the recovery of investment and the relaunch of the economy (Banco de Portugal 2017). Some measures have a potential impact on NPL reduction, such as the creation of an early warning mechanism by IAPMEI (a specialised public agency supporting Portuguese SMEs), which provides information on the economic and financial situation of companies, to avoid situations in which the non-financial firms in distress postpone taking restructuring measures that may prevent additional difficulties in the future (and their insolvency in the worst-case scenario). A second measure is the creation of a framework for converting loans to a commercial company into share capital, under the terms of which the creditors may propose to the company the conversion of their loans into share capital, upon verification of certain conditions (namely, the company's own funds are lower than the share capital, and the company's non-subordinated credit past due by over 90 days accounts for more than 10 per cent of the total non-subordinated credit). This measure particularly benefits non-financial companies in distress, which need to strengthen their capital structure. A third measure is the creation of the out-of-court regime for corporate recovery (Regime Extrajudicial de Recuperação de Empresas [RERE]), which replaces the out-of-court corporate recovery system (Sistema de Recuperação de Empresas por via Extrajudicial [SIREVE]), through which a debtor in financial distress or in an imminent insolvency situation may begin negotiations with all or some of its creditors with a view to reaching an agreement—voluntary and generally confidential—promoting its recovery (Lei n. 8/2018). The lessons learnt from the functioning of the SIREVE showed the importance of making the out-of-court corporate recovery process as streamlined as possible, preferably also giving it the tax and fees relief that the special revitalisation proceedings (Processo Especial de Revitalização [PER]) already benefit from. The PER basically allows the debtor to have a moratorium from creditors while he or she tries to agree a recovery plan with them. Fourth, the Corporate Recovery Mediator's statute, responsible for providing assistance to a debtor company in financial distress or in an insolvency situation, could complement the RERE procedure, especially in negotiations with creditors to reach an out-of-court restructuring agreement. The measure has the goal of increasing the success rate of corporate recovery and restructuring processes by providing support through mediators to the debtor company when negotiating with the creditors. Finally, a Single Window (Balcão Único) for the integrated management of Social Security and Portuguese Tax Authority credits to companies in the framework of insolvency proceedings has been approved (Article 5 of Law No. 100/2017 of 28 August 2017 refers to this initiative, but leaves the possibility of creating this Single Window to regulation by Decree Law). This measure aims to streamline the interaction between the different public creditors involved in non-financial firms' restructuring and insolvency proceedings.

Moreover, the Portuguese government promoted other changes in legislation to support the swift reduction of NPL stock. In particular, it created a framework for appropriating the pledged asset under commercial pledge, through which the parties may agree, if the collateral provider is a merchant, that the creditor, in the case of default, appropriates the pledged good or right for the value that results from its appraisal (the so-called Martian pact).[3] Similarly to a measure recently introduced into Italian jurisdiction, this measure is designed to expedite the processes for appropriating assets by creditors and is only applicable to new credits.

3.2.3.2   The Second Pillar

The second pillar is the microprudential supervision under the SSM. In the context of the SSM, the Banco de Portugal defined the reduction of the high NPL ratio in the Portuguese banking sector as one of the main supervisory priorities since 2016. Thus, a set of initiatives was defined to address this vulnerability in the sector, deepening some of the measures taken in previous years and strengthening supervisory action in monitoring banks' asset quality. These initiatives were designed specifically for institutions with a higher NPL level. For instance, one of the measures promoted under the SSM is the dialogue with the banks and the audit firms with a view to raising awareness of prudential concerns and the supervisory perspective, while also discussing solution strategies and monitoring the results achieved by the institutions. Other measures, in common with all euro area countries, are the request of granular information on NPLs, by the Banco de Portugal for less significant institutions and by the ECB for significant institutions and the monitoring of compliance with NPL reduction plans presented by banks and with the ECB guidance to banks on non-performing loans (Banco de Portugal 2017).

3.2.3.3   The Third Pillar

The third and last pillar is the management of the NPL portfolios, including possible systemic measures. While the first and second pillars of the strategy to address the NPL stock in Portugal are supported by measures adopted by the government (legal, judicial and fiscal components) and by the supervisor (under the SSM), the third pillar is expected to arise from banks' initiative, alongside the necessary coordination with the other entities involved in the overall strategy. The management of NPL portfolios is effectively the responsibility of the banks that hold them, within the framework previously detailed. The banks may choose between various alternatives to manage them, from those that include keeping the assets on the balance sheet, if accompanied by measures helping them to transform into performing assets, to selling them, including also the possible securitisation of this type of asset (Banco de Portugal 2018).

In the case of Portugal, a possible solution designed for the domestic banking system in general has been assessed, not only because of the high NPL stock but also because of the complexity of debtors' positions, as many debtors have received credit from several banks.

Because of the existence of asset segments that might require differentiated solutions, a bulk transfer of almost all the NPLs in the banking system to an asset management company, as has happened in other European countries in recent years, was excluded. Indeed, the homogeneity of the transferred assets seems to be one of the key success factors of an asset management company. Furthermore, a bulk transfer had to take into account the banks' capital and funding. On the first aspect, assuming an entirely private solution, it is necessary to consider the price that the investors, who support the asset management company, are willing to pay for NPLs and the consequent impact that the transfer of a significant volume of assets might have on the banks' balance sheet. As for funding, since a private solution is subject to the above-mentioned constraint, the state's involvement could be considered in order to reduce the balance sheet impact of such a transfer, for instance in the form of the state taking a holding in the asset management company itself or a guarantee for its funding. However, this solution is an intervention from the Portuguese state, with inevitable repercussions for the public accounts. The regulatory framework of the European Union, in the case of the creation of an asset management company with some type of state support, is still demanding, even if the adoption of the Blueprint for the potential set-up of national asset management companies has simplified the rules.

3.2.3.4 The Platform for Integrated Management of Bank Loans

As most Portuguese companies received credit from several banks, efforts were redirected towards promoting a greater creditor coordination to accelerate credit restructuring and/or NPL sales. In 2017, the Platform for Integrated Management of Bank Loans (Plataforma de Gestão de Créditos Bancários [ACE]) came to light in this context, comprising a complementary grouping of companies resulting from a joint initiative between Caixa Geral de Depósitos, Millennium BCP and Novo Banco, which aims to provide integrated management of credit granted to debtors to various banks (cross-exposures), which will remain on the balance sheet of the banks in question. The Platform has not led to a sharp reduction in the NPLs of the banking system in the short term, as it does not involve a transfer of assets off the banks' balance sheet. However, it contributes to the overall NPL reduction effort. Indeed, the Platform aims to improve credit recovery operations and speed up the process of reducing NPLs in the banks' portfolio, to assist with the recovery of Portuguese economic sectors, through restructuring of loans and debtors, to facilitate the access of companies that are being restructured to financing sources for fresh equity and to accelerate the negotiation process of creditors and banks, with the aim of restructuring companies (Caixa Geral de Depósitos 2017).

Aside from the benefits of greater creditor coordination and restructuring of viable companies, the Platform presents the additional advantage of being able to complement other initiatives under the overall NPL reduction strategy. In particular, as it addresses a specific set of assets—credit classified as NPLs that the involved credit institutions hold over common debtors—it does not preclude solutions that may be developed for other segments of non-productive assets held by the credit institutions (Banco de Portugal 2018).

As a final remark, while it is true that the measures to be adopted by the banks in their NPL reduction strategies should avoid fire sales, with a potentially negative impact on the banking sector and on economic activity, it is also true that the solution for some assets must involve their timely sale or their active and effective management. Against this backdrop, the distinction between different types of assets and thus between different types of solution is extremely important.

3.2.4   Italy

Figure 3.5 shows that while the gross amount of loans and advances increased by 4 per cent from 2014 to 2017, the gross NPL amount decreased by 32 per cent. Although this trend cannot be attributed to

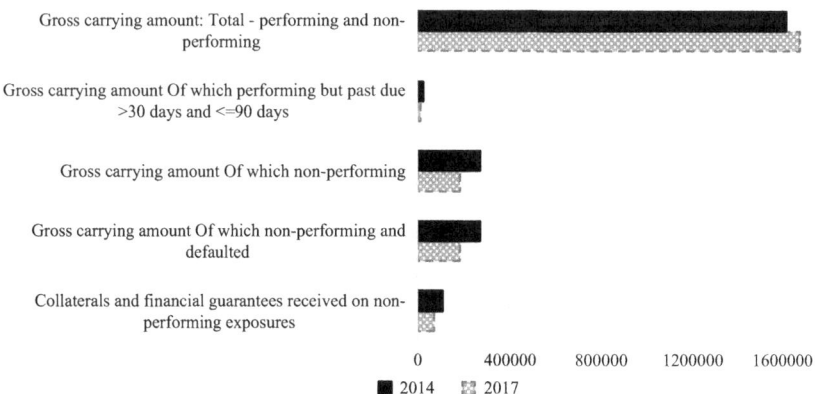

Fig. 3.5   Loans and advances in Italy (euro million). Source: Author's elaboration on EBA (2015, 2018) available at: https://eba.europa.eu/risk-analysis-and-data/eu-wide-transparency-exercise/2018

each specific reform, overall it signifies an improved quality of loan portfolios in Italian banks, mainly thanks to securitisation and sales on the market (35 and 65 billion euro gross in 2017 and 2018, respectively).

3.2.4.1 Drivers of NPL Reduction

According to Angelini (2018), the decreasing trend of NPLs can be explained by various factors. First, it reflects a cyclical improvement, which has helped to reduce the amount of new NPLs to similar or lower amounts than those observed before 2008 and has had a positive effect on the prices of positions with collateral, mostly in the form of real estate.

Second, the legislative changes introduced in 2015 and 2016 to speed up foreclosure proceedings had a positive effect.

Third, the ability to sell and the price of sale can vary significantly depending on the quality of the data that the seller is able to make available to potential buyers. Thus, the Italian supervisor contributed to this improvement in January 2016 by asking the banks for a detailed statistical report on bad debts.

Finally, structural changes in the market enhanced sales of NPLs. A number of banks have decided to specialise in NPL purchase and recovery. In 2018, five specialised less significant banks had 1.3 billion euro of NPLs on their balance sheets (700 million euro in 2016), corresponding to 20 billion euro in gross terms (12 billion euro in 2016). These banks also act as managers, that is, the so-called servicer, which is materially responsible for recovering the value from the portfolio being sold. There is also a specialisation by NPL type (consumer credit, business loans, covered or uncovered, etc.). On average, these specialised banks show a double-digit return on capital, which is in line with the Bank of Italy's expectations. The book value of Italian banks' bad debts is, on average, in line with the values that the banks in fact manage to recover.

As for non-bank financial intermediaries, at the end of 2017, there were 16 specialised intermediaries listed on the special register created pursuant to Article 106 of the Consolidated Law on Banking (Testo Unico Bancario [TUB]), which were involved in buying and selling NPLs. The NPLs on their balance sheets had a net value of 680 million euro. In this sector there were also nine companies that specialised in servicing NPL securitisation, of which three belonged to banking groups. The total amount of securitised loans managed by these companies was 28 billion euro in 2017 (+55 per cent compared with 2016). The sector of investment funds actively dealing in NPLs is also expanding. In the crisis years there were few of these funds, and they were mainly non-European, while by mid-2018 there were 21 Italian credit funds that had invested about 3 billion euro of the net wealth in NPLs.

As regards market techniques, there has been a growth in securitisation and related transactions involving a significant transfer of risk. Several transactions featured the sale of both the NPL portfolio and the servicing platform; in some cases, banks retained an interest in the platform. The observed transfer prices range from 16 to over 40 per cent of the gross portfolio value due to the different quality of the underlying portfolio, in particular to the share of collateralised positions, type of collateral, age of positions, size and the differing conditions both of the market and of the individual originator. For example, more recent transactions tend to benefit from a more mature market, while banks in difficulty may be penalised in negotiations.

There are also differences in the amounts sold, which range from a minimum of a few hundred million euro to a maximum of 24 billion euro, mainly depending on the size of the bank. The thickness of the senior tranches of securitisation was between 60 and 90 per cent of the net value of the portfolio being sold. There is often a mezzanine tranche. Junior tranches accounted for between 3 and 13 per cent of the net value sold, mainly depending on whether mezzanine tranches were available.

A rating for the senior tranche was obtained in most transactions, partly because it is a necessary condition for the state guarantee (GACS—explained below). Banks often keep the junior and mezzanine tranches at the minimum required by law, which is 5 per cent. The maximum limit on the portion of these tranches to be retained is not explicit, but rather implicit in order to obtain the deconsolidation of the securitised portfolio, an essential objective of the banks that carry out this kind of transaction. Although the total retention of the senior tranche was observed in most cases, in others, shares of up to 75 per cent of the tranche were placed on the market (Angelini 2018). In most transactions, the securities issued by the securitisation vehicle were purchased by a single investor. In all the operations observed so far, servicers are independent of banks as independence is a requirement for the GACS. The rating agencies also evaluate how good a transaction is on the basis of the characteristics and reputation of the servicers.

3.2.4.2   The Italian Guarantee on Securitisation of Bank Non-performing Loans

The Italian Guarantee on Securitisation of Bank Non-Performing Loans (GACS) provides for the granting of state guarantees as part of securitisation transactions whose underlying assets are non-performing loans. The state shall guarantee only the senior tranches of securitisation transactions and the riskiest tranches (junior and mezzanine) shall not be repaid until the senior tranches have been fully repaid. Guarantees may be requested by banks that securitise and sell their non-performing loans, against regular payment of a fee to the Treasury, calculated as a yearly percentage of the amount guaranteed. The price of the guarantee is a market price, as recognised by the European Commission, which agrees that the scheme does not envisage any state aid. The price shall be calculated on the basis of a single-name CDS (Credit Default Swap) related to Italian issuers with a risk level equal to that of the guaranteed securities. The price increases in time, both to cover for the higher risk associated with a longer duration of the bonds and to incorporate into the scheme a strong incentive to recover the credit early. The price for the first three years is calculated as an average of the mid-price of three-year benchmark CDS for issuers with a rating equal to that of the guaranteed tranches. In the fourth and fifth years the price increases after the first step up (five-year CDS) and an incentivising premium will be paid to offset the lower rate paid for the first three years. From the sixth year onwards the guarantee is fully priced (seven-year CDS). In the sixth and seventh year an additional incentivising premium is paid to offset the lower rate paid for the first five years. The state issues the guarantee only after the securities have received a rating equal to or higher than the investment grade from an independent rating agency included in the list of credit rating agencies accepted by the Eurosystem (MEF 2016). Banks completed 21 transactions using the GACS state guarantee scheme, securitising more than 62 billion euro in bad loans. The GACS has, therefore, been extended for two years starting in March 2019, albeit under stricter conditions. For instance, under the new scheme, senior notes in bad loan securitisations tapping the state guarantee must be rated at least at Baa2 versus the Baa3 previously allowed (Reuters 2019).

The government also established Atlante in 2016, a private fund whose primary role was to inject capital into Italian banks through share purchases, in order to stabilise the domestic financial system.[4] In addition to providing capital infusions, Atlante was mandated with buying junior tranches of securitised NPLs. A second fund—the Italian Recovery Fund (previously called Atlante II)—was subsequently rolled out when its predecessor's capital was swiftly depleted, although the new fund's role was narrower, tasked exclusively with helping banks securitise their NPLs (Dimarco 2018).

The overall effect of this series of cyclical and structural developments, set against the sharp increase in the supply of NPLs on the market, and therefore of sales, is that prices have been almost stable. Recoveries by sale yielded an average of 23 per cent of the gross value in 2017 and 2016, compared to 20 per cent in 2015 (Conti et al. 2017). The Bank of Italy evaluates each transaction on a case-by-case basis to assess whether there has been a significant transfer of risk and it is commensurate with the capital relief, avoiding regulatory arbitrage.[5]

3.3   CONCLUSION

In line with the post-crisis regulatory improvements, banks and other market participants have acquired substantial knowledge and experience in resolving NPLs. The steady growth in NPL sales and NPL securitisation has encouraged this important evolution towards a more mature NPL resolution environment. Yet a truly sustainable solution for the remaining NPL problem in Europe depends on putting further effort into innovative and collaborative approaches. Some are already emerging in the market, as comprehensive partnerships have been taking shape between different market participants, for instance between banks and specialised third-party servicers. This increasingly allows them to share knowledge and information. In this way, banks and other market players are able to make further advances in digitalisation and platform initiatives (such as creditor coordination or data repositories). These developments have the potential to reduce the cost of NPL management and make it easier to transfer NPLs from banks to businesses that are better equipped to carry the relevant operational and financial burden. Continued specialisation among market participants may further improve efficiency in managing and resolving NPLs from different asset classes.

These improvements are crucial in order to address the current stock of NPLs effectively. So far, efforts have concentrated strongly on NPLs secured by collateral and—to a lesser extent—on unsecured retail NPLs. In the most exposed countries, a large portion of the remaining exposure consists of NPLs to corporate and small and medium-sized enterprises, which are more heterogeneous in nature and can often prove more complex to tackle.

Euro area countries analysed in this chapter show some common features in dealing with NPLs, such as the greater attention to the quality and flows of information, the introduction of securitisation schemes assisted by some form of state guarantee, under the provision of EU legislation, and the standardisation of policies and procedures on the resolution and closure of non-performing loans. As we have seen in this chapter, governments have also applied tailored strategies that best fit the domestic legislative and economic framework and adequately consider public opinion. For example, households' indebtedness and collateral recovery are of particular relevance in Cyprus, whereas they are not considered to be problematic in Italy. It is important that all euro area banks define and implement a reliable strategy to tackle NPL as further build-up can easily derive from a sudden economic downturn.

After focusing on NPLs, as one of the main obstacles preventing euro area banking systems from being profitable, in the next chapter two additional drivers of low profitability, namely Level 3 assets and sovereign exposure, are investigated.

NOTES

1. In 2013, the Resolution of Credit and Other Institutions Law 17(I)/2013 was enacted. It allowed the Resolution Authority of Cyprus (Central Bank of Cyprus) to take steps in order to maintain stability in the banking and financial services industry, and granted it the power to adopt and implement resolution measures regarding affected institutions. The Resolution Law was implemented ahead of EU Directive 2014/59/EU of the European Parliament and of the Council of 15 May 2014 because of the difficulties faced by Cypriot banks in 2013. The Resolution Law of 2013 was replaced by legislation enacted on 18 March 2016, namely Law 22(I)/2016 on the Regulation of the Resolution of Credit Institutions and Investment Companies and related matters for the purposes of harmonising the measures available under Cyprus law with those set out in Directive 2014/59/EU (Alexandrou et al. 2018).
2. The Immovable Property (Transfer and Mortgage) Law, No. 9/1965, as amended by Law 139(I)/2015 is part of the reform strategy. As for personal insolvency, provisions are set out in the Bankruptcy Law (Chapter 5) and the Bankruptcy Rules. In addition, the Insolvency of Individuals (Personal Repayment and Relief Plans) Law 65(I)/2015 provides for the handling of insolvent individuals. The Companies Law (Chapter 113) governs corporate

insolvency and reorganisation. In 2015, the Companies Law was amended to introduce the notion of examinership into Cyprus Law. As such, companies may be reorganised to meet their financial obligations. Furthermore, the Companies Law allows for corporate reorganisation, which under Section 30 of the Income Tax Law 118(I) of 2002 includes the following: merger, division, partial division, transfer of assets, exchange of shares and transfer of registered office. Certain provisions of the Bankruptcy Law regarding the rights of secured and unsecured creditors are also applicable to the winding up of insolvent companies (Alexandrou et al. 2018).

3. Decree Law No. 75/2017 of 26 June 2017.
4. Atlante is an Italian private equity fund that was dedicated to recapitalise some Italian banks, as well as purchase the securities of the junior tranches of non-performing loans. The fund was managed by Quaestio Capital Management SGR S.p.A., a wholly owned subsidiary of Quaestio Holding S.A., which was owned by Fondazione Cariplo (37.65%), Fondazione Cassa dei Risparmi di Forlì (6.75%), Cassa Italiana di Previdenza e Assistenza dei Geometri liberi professionisti (18%), Locke S.r.l. (22%) and Direzione Generale Opere Don Bosco (15.60%). Atlante's investors were 67 Italian and foreign Institutions, including banks, insurance companies, banking foundations and the Cassa Depositi e Prestiti. Although a full analysis of Atlante is outside the scope of this book, it was initially set up to help free Italy's banks of bad debt. Atlante could invest in banks with a lower capital ratio than the minimum established in the context of the SREP and that therefore, upon request by the Supervisory Authority, implement initiatives to reinforce capital by means of a share capital increase, and/or, in NPLs originating from a variety of Italian banks (Quaestio Capital Management 2019). It eventually made an offer to buy the impaired loans of three small banks that were rescued from bankruptcy in 2015 (Reuters 2016). It raised 4.25 billion euros from banks and insurers, as well as some funding from state-owned entities, but spent over half of that to recapitalise regional banks Popolare di Vicenza and Veneto Banca. A second fund (Atlante II) was subsequently created. The fund, renamed "Italian Recovery Fund" is involved in four securitisations of approximately euro 31 billion gross of NPLs, with an investment of about euro 2.5 billion. Established thanks to the commitment of Italian and international financial institutions, at a time of crisis in the Italian banking system to exclusively invest in the impaired loans, the Italian Recovery Fund is the largest investor dedicated to Italy's NPL market. It was involved in four securitisations of approximately euro 31 billion gross of NPLs (about half of the total euro 65 billion of operations estimated by the IMF for 2017 in Italy) with a total investment of about euro 2.5 billion.

Its presence in the market allowed to solve by means of divestments or recapitalisations, situations of bank crises, including Nuova Banca Marche, Nuova Banca dell'Etruria, Nuova Cassa di Risparmio di Chieti, Nuova Cassa di Risparmio di Ferrara, Banca MPS, Cassa di Risparmio di Cesena, Cassa di Risparmio di Rimini and Cassa di Risparmio di San Miniato.

5. In 2017, the EBA launched a public consultation and a discussion paper on the significant risk transfer in securitisation to better adapt the regulatory framework to the characteristics of securitisation transactions, especially those involving underlying NPLs, and to facilitate the harmonisation of supervisory practices.

References

Alexandrou, A., K. Stylianou, and A. Panagasidis. 2018. Restructuring and insolvency, Tornaritis Law Firm, December. https://gettingthedealthrough.com/area/35/jurisdiction/74/restructuring-insolvency-cyprus/.

Andreou, S., and C. Koutsampelas. 2019. The "Estia" scheme in Cyprus: A social policy mirage? ESPN Flash Report 2019/03.

Angelini, P. 2018. Non-performing loans: The market, the rules and a stronger system. Rome, October.

Banco de Portugal. 2017. Financial stability report, June 2017.

———. 2018. Financial stability report, December 2017.

Bank of Greece. 2014. Executive Committee Act 42/30.5.2014, Supervisory framework for the management of loans in arrears and non-performing loans.

———. 2015. Executive Committee Act 47/09.02.2015, Amendments to Executive Committee Act (ECA) 42/30.05.2014, Supervisory framework for the management of loans in arrears and non-performing loans – Repeal of Bank of Greece Administration's Circular 13/30.07.2009.

———. 2016. Executive Committee Act 102/30.8.2016, Amendment to the Act of the Executive Committee 42/30.05.2014. Prudential framework for the management of exposures in arrears and non-performing exposures.

———. 2018a. Executive Committee Act 134/05.03.2018, Amendment to the Act of the Executive Committee 42/30.05.2014, Prudential framework for the management of exposures in arrears and non performing exposures.

———. 2018b. Executive Committee Act 136/02.04.2018, Amendment to the Act of the Executive Committee 42/30.05.2014, Prudential framework for the management of exposures in arrears and non-performing exposures.

———. 2018c. Overview of the Greek financial system special feature, November.

———. 2019. Evolution of loans & non-performing loans. https://www.bankofgreece.gr/Pages/en/Statistics/loans.aspx.

Caixa Geral de Depósitos. 2017. Caixa Geral de Depósitos, Millennium bcp and Novo Banco agree to set up a platform for the integrated management of non-performing bank loans – Announcement. https://www.cgd.pt/English/Investor-Relations/Announcements/Material-Information/Documents/IP-28SET2017_ENG.pdf.

Conti, F.M., I. Guida, A. Rendina, and G. Santini. 2017. Bad loan recovery rates in 2016, Banca d'Italia, Notes on Financial Stability and Supervision, 11.

Dimarco, E. 2018. NPLs in Italy: A gradual unwind, Deutsche Bank corporate and investment banking flow, May 2018.

EBA. 2015. 2015 EU-wide transparency exercise. https://eba.europa.eu/risk-analysis-and-data/eu-wide-transparency-exercise/2015/results.

———. 2018. 2018 EU-wide transparency exercise. https://eba.europa.eu/risk-analysis-and-data/eu-wide-transparency-exercise/2018/results.

EC. 2018. Commission staff working document, accompanying the document communication from the Commission to the European parliament, the Council and the European Central Bank, Third Progress Report on the Reduction of Non-Performing Loans in Europe COM(2018) 766 final, SWD(2018) 472 final.

ECB. 2017. *Stocktake of national supervisory practices and legal frameworks related to NPLs*, June.

———. 2018. ECB *Annual report on supervisory activities 2018: Implementing the SSM model of supervision.*

Georgiopoulos, G., and L. Papadimas. 2019. Greece gets drastic on sour loans with securitisation schemes. *Reuters News*, February 20. https://uk.reuters.com/article/uk-greece-banks-loans-securitisation/greece-gets-drastic-on-sour-loans-with-securitisation-schemes-idUKKCN1Q91KF.

IMF. 2017. *Reforming the legal framework to support private debt restructuring, Cyprus: selected issues.* IMF Country Report No. 17/376, pp. 30–45, Washington.

———. 2018a. Financial soundness indicators. http://data.imf.org/?sk=51B096FA-2CD2-40C2-8D09-0699CC1764DA&sId=1390030341854.

———. 2018b. *Challenges in reducing NPL overhang and restoring credit financing, Cyprus: selected issues.* IMF Country Report No. 18/338, Washington.

Ministry of Economy and Finance. 2016. Definito lo strumento per facilitare lo smaltimento delle sofferenze bancarie: presto disponibile la Garanzia Cartolarizzazione Sofferenze (GACS), Comunicato Stampa 20 del 27/01/2016, Department of Treasury. http://www.mef.gov.it/ufficio-stampa/comunicati/2016/comunicato_0020.html.

Quaestio Capital Management. 2019. Atlante, alternative fund. https://www.quaestiocapital.com/en/about-us/.

Reuters. 2016. Update 1-Italian bank rescue fund Atlante to buy more bad loans. https://www.reuters.com/article/italy-banks-ma/update-1-italian-bank-rescue-fund-atlante-to-buy-more-bad-loans-idUSL8N1DN3LQ.

———. 2019. Renewal of Italian guarantee scheme credit positive for banks: Moody's, March 25. https://www.reuters.com/article/eurozone-banks-italy-bad-loans/renewal-of-italian-guarantee-scheme-credit-positive-for-banks-moodys-idUSL8N21C50D.

Rutter Pooley, C., and R. Smith. 2018. Bank of Cyprus sells €2.7bn bad loans to Apollo. *Financial Times*, August 28. https://www.ft.com/content/25cb5846-aa8b-11e8-89a1-e5de165fa619.

CHAPTER 4

Level 3 Assets and Sovereign Exposure

4.1 Introduction

This chapter first revises the state of the art on Level 3 assets, the second major driver of fragility for the EU banking system. European authorities have mainly focused on fragility from credit risks, but the global financial crisis highlighted the importance of correctly pricing highly complex and opaque instruments, to avoid risk contagion, unjustified profits and regulatory capital relief. In this respect, the crisis started a trend towards simplification and transparency, entailing a radical change in banks' business models.

Then the chapter focuses on the linkage between sovereign debt and bank balance sheets. The home bias problem is also a key obstacle to the adoption of a European Deposit Insurance Scheme (EDIS), as proposed by the European Commission in late 2015, because deposits protected by this scheme might be used by banks, under moral suasion from their home country's government, to excessively increase their purchases of that government's debt. As a response to this, policymakers are now discussing whether and how to address the treatment of sovereign debt on bank balance sheets, which is currently treated as risk free. Banks do not need to set aside capital to protect themselves from potential losses in sovereign securities and do not have any limits on their exposure to a particular sovereign. This chapter investigates two proposed options to address this issue: applying non-zero risk weights to sovereign exposures and putting limits on exposures to sovereigns, similar to those in place for other exposures.

© The Author(s) 2019   67
F. Arnaboldi, *Risk and Regulation in Euro Area Banks*, Palgrave
Macmillan Studies in Banking and Financial Institutions,
https://doi.org/10.1007/978-3-030-23429-4_4

4.2   Level 3 Assets

Level 3 assets (L3) are financial instruments whose fair value needs some form of estimation, as it cannot be directly observed from prices in active markets (Banca d'Italia 2017). L3 (and L2) assets may constitute a major risk for financial stability, as they are hard to quantitatively evaluate and liquidate. Their fair value cannot be determined using directly observable market data but can only be priced using complex and discretionary internal models. Despite progress towards simplification and transparency, there is still complexity in the balance sheets of the major banks in the euro area.

Before specifically addressing the L3 issue, it is worthwhile to illustrate the difference between L1, L2 and L3 assets. All these instruments should be valued at fair value (FV).[1] The starting point for FV measurement is a quoted price in an active market, if available. A market is active if transactions take place with sufficient frequency and volume to provide meaningful pricing information on an ongoing basis. As these conditions are not always met, the *International Financial Reporting Standard 13* (IFRS 13) adopts the following hierarchy for parameters that enter the valuation mechanism of a FV instrument: L1 parameters are prices quoted for that specific instrument in an active market at the measurement date; L2 parameters are valuation inputs that are observable, either directly or indirectly; and L3 parameters are unobservable, that is, market data on these inputs are either not available or not sufficiently reliable (Banca d'Italia 2017).[2]

Financial instruments are classified into three categories depending on the hierarchical level of the inputs that are significant in their valuation. This methodology allows for instruments of the same type to end up in different categories, given that only the specific features of each contract determine which parameters are actually relevant.[3]

These few lines clarify that uncertainties in measurement and classification of L3 assets are significant. Table 4.1 describes a sample of about 120 large euro area banks from Orbis Bank in 2017.

The estimated total amount of L3 assets in 2017 was higher than 1 trillion euro, compared to 786 billion euro of non-performing loans (NPLs) (Table 4.2).[4] As in the case of NPL, described in Chaps. 2 and 3, euro area countries under scrutiny present heterogeneous features. Three countries, France, Spain and Germany, cover 81 per cent of the total amount of L3 assets in the banks under scrutiny. The distribution of these assets is highly concentrated in a few countries, as it is for NPLs. Indeed, the first three

Table 4.1 Sample description

Country	No. Banks
Austria	5
Belgium	7
Cyprus	1
Germany	17
Spain	13
Finland	3
France	35
Greece	4
Ireland	5
Italy	15
Luxembourg	3
Netherlands	6
Portugal	5
Total	119

Source: Authors' elaboration on Orbis Bank data

Table 4.2 Level 3 assets data—euro area (2017)

Country	Level 3 assets (fair value hierarchy)[a] (euro million)	Total impaired/ Non-performing loans (euro million)	Level 3 assets/ Securities (%)	Level 3 assets/ Common Equity Tier 1 (CET1) capital (%)
	Total by country		Average by country	
Austria	92,744	12,839	49.2	454.3
Belgium	34,798	14,857	10.9	72.9
Cyprus	18	1714	0.6	na
Germany	223,510	37,593	13.9	280.9
Spain	305,382	114,685	18.7	313.8
Finland	2354	6522	4.6	23.8
France	352,729	207,640	20.8	284.2
Greece	352	94,454	1.7	1.1
Ireland	3842	20,922	5.8	12.0
Italy	11,140	225,423	2.3	8.7
Luxembourg	766	1080	3.6	6.3
Netherlands	5493	37,452	1.7	6.3
Portugal	52,794	10,456	33.4	282.4
All euro area countries	1,085,923	785,639	15.0	191.3

Source: Authors' elaboration on Orbis Bank data

Note: Northern countries are Austria, Belgium, Finland, Germany, Ireland, Luxembourg and Netherlands. Southern countries are Cyprus, France, Greece, Italy, Portugal and Spain

[a]Orbis Bank defines Level 3 assets (fair value hierarchy) as Total level 3 valuation of financial assets (market-based measurement)

countries in terms of NPLs, namely Italy, France and Spain, account for 70 per cent of total NPLs of the sample.

Further differences among euro area countries emerge when comparing Northern and Southern countries' L3 assets and NPL amounts. Northern countries bear 33 per cent of total L3 assets and only 17 per cent of NPLs. As Banca d'Italia (2017) states, the frequency and magnitude of the unexpected negative returns for L3 assets can be considered as comparable with those for NPL. However, if NPLs are an issue mainly for Southern euro area countries, L3 assets appear to be more concentrated in France and Germany. Figure 4.1 reports data from EBA at the end of 2017 for global systemically important institutions and other large institutions with an overall exposure measure of more than 200 billion euro.[5]

It is also clear that placing greater emphasis on the assessment of credit risk underlying the portfolios of commercial banks, rather than on market risk underlying securities portfolios of wholesale banks, represents a regulatory bias favouring some banks—and some countries—rather than others. As Fig. 4.2 illustrates, in 2017 the amount of L3 assets reported by five G-SII banks is larger than the total amount of L3 assets reported by all other G-SII banks of the EBA (2018c) sample (73.1 vs. 67.1 billion euro).

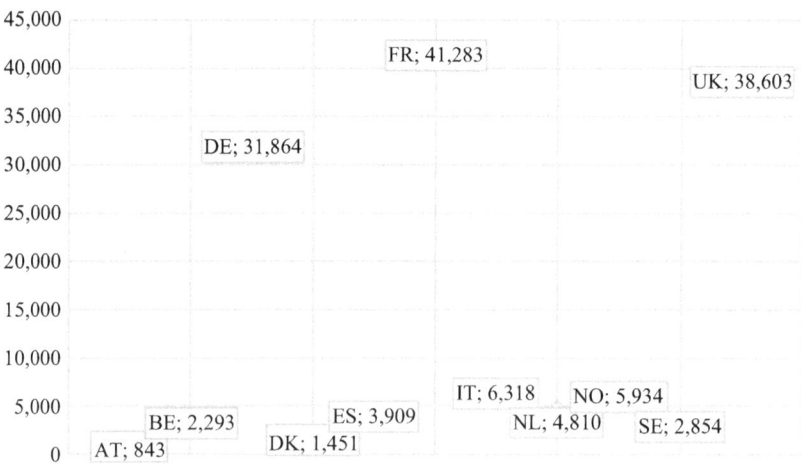

Fig. 4.1 Level 3 assets (euro million) in 2017 by country. Source: Author's elaboration on EBA (2018c)

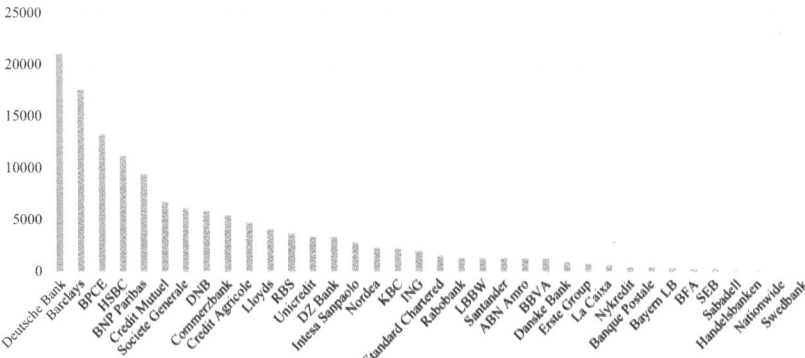

Fig. 4.2 Level 3 assets (euro million) in 2017 by bank. Source: Author's elaboration on EBA (2018c)

Limiting the investigation to the seven euro area countries in the EBA (2018c) sample, namely Austria, Belgium, France, Germany, Italy, the Netherlands and Spain, from 2013 to 2017, the total value of L3 assets decreased by 25 per cent (Fig. 4.3). Nevertheless, L3 assets reported by Austrian banks increased by 155 per cent, as compared to −55 per cent for Italian banks and −36 per cent for Belgian banks. Spanish banks' L3 assets remain almost stable in the 5 years under scrutiny (−3 per cent). French and German G-SII banks reduced their exposure by about one-fifth.

As shown in Table 4.2, the magnitude of these assets is relevant, compared to the size of the securities portfolio and, in particular, to banks' capitalisation. Again, differences among countries are striking: L3 assets amount to about 50 per cent of the securities portfolio for Austrian banks in the sample, 33 per cent for Portuguese banks and 21 per cent for France banks, as opposed to 0.6 per cent of the securities portfolio for Cypriot banks, and 1.7 per cent for Greek and Dutch banks. Austrian banks would be particularly under pressure if some kind of downturn causes a collapse in the prices of these products, as the ratio of L3 assets to CET1 is higher than 100 per cent. Spain, France, Portugal and Germany show similar three-digit ratios. Greece, Italy, Luxembourg and the Netherlands, in contrast, show an average L3-to-CET1 ratio lower than 10 per cent.

L3 assets can be classified into various portfolios as other kinds of securities. Figure 4.4 shows the estimated amount held for each category: trading (HFT), held to maturity (HTM), available for sale (AFS), and other, and the total amount of L3.

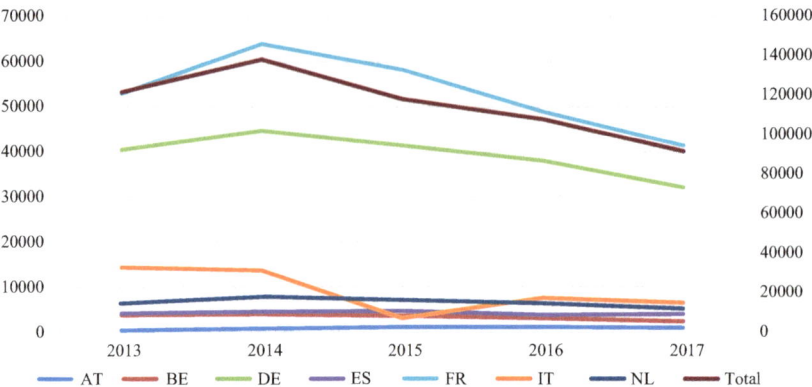

Fig. 4.3 Level 3 assets (euro million)—time trend. Source: Author's elaboration on EBA (2018c). Note: Countries' L3 assets values are reported on the left-hand Y axis; the total value of L3 assets for the countries under scrutiny is reported on the right-hand Y axis

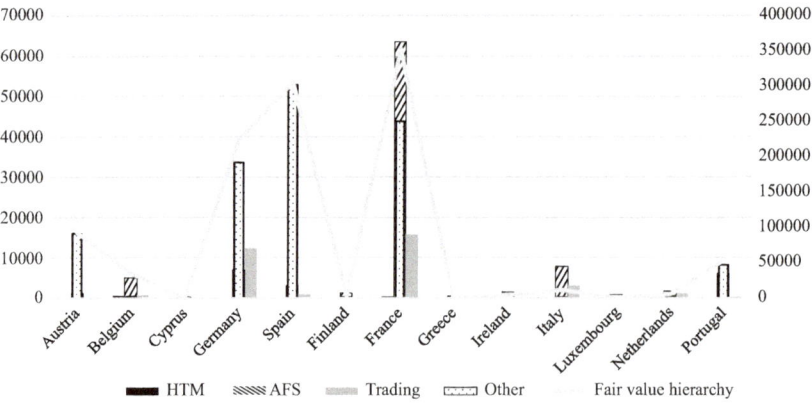

Fig. 4.4 Level 3 assets (euro million). Source: Authors' elaboration on Orbis Bank data. Note: Level 3 asset—other and Level 3 asset Fair value hierarchy are represented on the right end Y axis. Level 3 financial assets—HFT: includes all trading assets measured at fair value using Level 3 technique (unobservable inputs); Level 3 financial assets—AFS: includes all available for sale assets measured at fair value using Level 3 technique (unobservable inputs); Level 3 financial assets—HTM: includes all held to maturity assets measured at fair value using Level 3 technique (unobservable inputs); Level 3 financial assets—other: includes all other assets measured at fair value using Level 3 technique (unobservable inputs); Level 3 assets (fair value hierarchy): total level 3 valuation of financial assets (market-based measurement) (Orbis Bank definitions)

The main category is the L3–other, which covers 82 per cent of the total value of this kind of asset, followed at great distance by L3–trading (3 per cent). L3–other is a residual classification which confirms the uncertainties in L3 measurement and classification and the discretion used in pricing these assets. Furthermore, the combination of L3 classification (HFT, HTM, AFS and other), fair value hierarchy and pricing may interact with the determination of the regulatory capital allocated.

Even if IFRS 13 contains disclosure requirements to provide transparency about the L3 assets' risks, and the valuation adjustments should be used to determine a fair and conservative valuation, this is not always the case. For example, the accounting principle requires valuations to be adjusted for liquidity risk, but it does not provide a binding solution for the adjustment method to use, or the size of the adjustment. Banks are required to implement a structured approach to FV measurement, but this entails making assumptions and having discretion on whether to value instruments at the individual or the portfolio level; whether or not to deem the reference markets active; and whether or not to consider certain inputs as significant. As a result, two banks with different degrees of conservativeness may decide to treat the same financial asset in different ways and end up with different valuations. In addition, banks may have incentives to use their discretion to distort the valuation process and the allocation of financial assets among the various categories, for several reasons: to recognise uncertain profits immediately, to reduce the fair value adjustments even in the absence of an active market and to maintain a good reputation among peers.[6] Thus the profits registered from certain complex transactions might in fact be named as a premium for a (hidden) risk.

4.2.1   Regulatory and Prudential Framework

The complexity of L3 assets valuation is duly acknowledged in the prudential framework. ECB (2014) provides the detailed instructions required to carry out the L3 fair value exposures review. The review has the aim of ensuring that the bank can appropriately evaluate the fair value of positions accounted for under the classifications available for sale, designated at fair value through P&L, and held for trading. ECB (2014) focuses on areas where misstatement of positions is most likely, and where such an event may have a material impact on the bank's overall CET1 ratio.

The supervisory goal is to assess both L3 FV volatility and reliability risk. The volatility risk, that is the risk of uncertain returns due to changes in market conditions and prices, is the target of capital requirements for market risks (e.g. RWA of the regulatory trading book). FV reliability risk, instead, reflects the extent to which the assumptions underlying FV measurement leave room for uncertainty. On this second type of risk, the Capital Requirements Regulation (575/2013, Articles 34 and 105) and EBA (2015a) require banks to compute a prudent valuation of all FV positions. The prudent valuation should proxy for the expected orderly exit price of an instrument, taking into account, interalia, bank-specific factors which are ruled out in the accounting valuation but may influence the exit price of a position (Banca d'Italia 2017). The difference between the FV and the prudent valuation, which is labelled Additional Valuation Adjustment (AVA), measures the potential downside risk and must be deducted from CET1.

EBA (2018a) adds the liquidity and model uncertainty shock on banks' reserves covering L2 and L3 to the 2018 stress test methodology. The shocks provided in the market risk scenario are applied to the bid-ask spread of L2 and L3 instruments and produce an increase in the reserves on fair value adjustments covering liquidity issues and model risk. Regarding the adjustments to AVA reserves, only those related to market price uncertainty, close-out cost and model risk are considered. The total impact coming from the model uncertainty shock on L3 assets amounts to −5.4 billion euro and affects capital mainly through profit and loss (EBA 2018b). Data projected by banks exhibit a high dispersion in terms of losses, with a range from −75 bps to almost zero. This high dispersion resembles the distribution of L3 assets among G-SII banks as reported in Fig. 4.2. Unfortunately, the AVA adjustment to CET1 builds on the same basic framework that is used for accounting FV adjustments; hence it may not fully address valuation concerns on L3 assets.

On the same note, BIS (2019a) adds L3 assets in the data collection exercise, which represents an input into the methodology to assess the systemic importance of banks in a global context. This methodology for identifying global systemically important banks is outlined in the July 2018 document titled "Global systemically important banks: revised assessment methodology and the higher loss absorbency requirement" (BIS 2018), and it is used by EBA (2018c). BIS (2018) responds to the decision by the G20 leaders to develop a methodology comprising both quantitative and qualitative indicators that can contribute to the assessment of the systemic importance of financial institutions at a global level and has been promoted by the Financial Stability Board.

Furthermore, the Basel Committee on Banking Supervision recently finalised a fundamental review of the trading book to enhance the prudential framework for market risk (BIS 2019b). This document sets out the amended minimum capital requirements for market risk that will serve as the Pillar 1 minimum capital requirement as of 1 January 2022, replacing the current minimum capital requirements for market risk as set out in Basel III and its subsequent amendments. It includes the following key changes: a simplified standardised approach for use by banks that have small or non-complex trading portfolios; clarifications on the scope of exposures that are subject to market risk capital requirements; refined standardised approach treatments of foreign exchange risk and index instruments; revised standardised approach risk weights applicable to the general interest rate risk, foreign exchange and certain exposures subject to credit spread risk; revisions to the assessment process to determine whether a bank's internal risk management models appropriately reflect the risks of individual trading desks; and revisions to the requirements for identification of risk factors that are eligible for internal modelling (BIS 2019c). As for L3 assets, the document improves the interdependence between the accounting and the prudential perspectives, improving both the regulatory booking and the capital requirement quantification; it might also have beneficial effects on the soundness and reliability of fair value measurement.

In sum, L3 instruments are subject to valuation uncertainty, potentially inherent to both sides of the balance sheet (assets and liabilities). Indeed, mispricing might consist in both inflated asset values and deflated liability values. Risks can be hedged as long as L3 instruments on the asset side are perfectly matched by instruments on the liability side, or vice versa. However, hedges are seldom perfect, especially in the case of complex positions. This brief investigation of the accounting and prudential framework suggests that much has already been done by supervisory authorities to strengthen the valuation process for L3 assets, but there is still room for improvement. In particular, the accounting framework requires banks to make assumptions and discretionary decisions in key areas of FV measurement, and this should be limited. For instance, L1 instruments are those traded in active markets, but accounting standards provide a definition of active markets which is difficult to apply. Deciding when a market is active entails some discretion of the bank holding the instrument. Second, as far as the prudential treatment is concerned, even if AVA is an important step forward, it does not fully solve the problem. Since banks have various incentives to use discretion to their advantage, L3 assets can be represented so as to minimise the associated capital charges and to augment the estimated trading profits.

4.3   SOVEREIGN DEBT EXPOSURE

After investigating two of the main sources of risk for euro area banks, namely NPL and L3 assets, and before moving to the Banking Union project in Chaps. 5 and 6, the home bias problem is now examined. The home bias problem generally refers to the highly concentrated sovereign exposures of euro area banks in the home country. A number of recent contributions have argued that banks should be discouraged from holding too much government debt and in particular should be discouraged from holding too much debt of their own government (Gennaioli et al. 2014; Korte and Steffen 2014; ESRB 2015; Andritzky et al. 2016). Sovereign risk, however, is not a novel concept. Sovereign defaults, though not as frequent as those in the private sector, have occurred regularly throughout history. The global financial crisis and subsequent distress suffered by a number of sovereigns, including some EU Member States, have further highlighted these risks. Indeed, the bond spreads and credit default swap (CDS) premiums observed for a number of sovereigns suggest that the possibility of default is clearly non-negligible (ESRB 2015). The crisis has also highlighted a close two-way link between banking and sovereign distress, with problems in the banking sector having a negative effect on sovereign issues, and sovereign stress exacerbating the disruption in the banking system. While a significant portion of sovereign bonds are classified as held to collect under the IFRS 9 accounting standard and do not therefore affect a bank's regulatory capital, a drop in the price of government bonds directly affects the perceived solvency of domestic banks, negatively affecting their market capitalisation thereby deteriorating their creditworthiness and their cost of funding (Sironi 2018).

Home bias is also considered an obstacle to the adoption of the EDIS, as proposed by the European Commission in late 2015 because deposits protected by such a scheme might be used by banks, under moral suasion from their home country's government, to excessively increase their purchases of that government's debt (Veron 2017). In turn, the absence of a full EDIS is one of the Banking Union's greatest weaknesses because deposits are not protected uniformly, as investigated in Chaps. 6 and 7.

Interestingly, the debate on domestic sovereign exposure is not new. Initially it took place in the early 1980s, when Basel I was crafted (Visco 2015). Two proposals were eventually put forward, one recommending a 20 per cent risk weight on domestic sovereign exposures and the other a zero-risk weight. Eventually the solution to apply a zero-risk weight was chosen, recognising the crucial role of sovereign bonds and securities in the functioning of financial markets, with the aim of fostering the development of domestic bond markets and the desire to avoid interference with fiscal and monetary policy. Nowadays, the mere recognition that there is no truly risk-free asset does not per se warrant a change in the regulatory treatment of sovereign exposures. A key counterargument is that the potential benefits of a reform are uncertain, while the potential costs could be sizeable. A prudent stance would be to wait for the financial system to fully recover and adapt to the important set of reforms implemented since the onset of the crisis before making further changes. This debate is further addressed at the end of this section.

4.3.1 Data on Sovereign Debt Exposure in the Euro Area Countries

In general, home bias increased in the euro area countries during the crisis and then progressively diminished. Figure 4.5 exhibits the gross amount of domestic debt securities held by each country's banks in 2013 and 2017. Italian banks had the largest exposure to domestic debt in 2013, higher than 220 billion euro, followed by French (almost 200 billion euro), Spanish (about 190 billion euro) and German banks (more than 180 billion euro). Though all banking systems reduced their home bias from 2013 to 2017, Italian banks nevertheless reduced their exposure by 50 per cent, as compared to French and Spanish banks, which were able to cut their domestic exposure to a lesser extent (42 and 38 per cent, respectively). Apart from Luxembourgish banks, which basically cancelled their domestic exposure (−94 per cent in the 4-year time period), Cypriot banks were the most effective in the euro area, as they reduced their exposure by 70 per cent.

At the end of 2017, in absolute terms, Spanish, Italian and French banks still exhibited the highest exposure to sovereign debt, larger than 100 billion euro (Fig. 4.6). Considering the overall debt securities portfolio held by banks, however, credit institutions in these countries have less than 40 per cent of their debt securities portfolio invested in domestic assets. Their portfolio is thus less concentrated than those of Cypriot, Greek and Portuguese banks, for instance (71.8, 57.9 and 55.5 per cent, respectively, of domestic exposure to total exposure ratio).

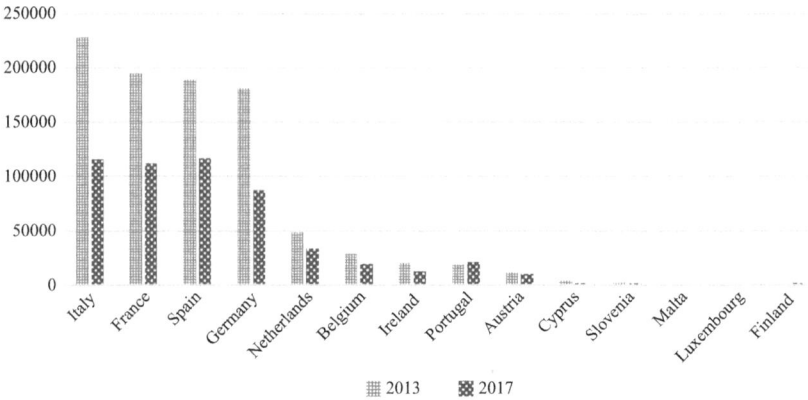

Fig. 4.5   Gross amount of sovereign debt securities domestic exposure (euro million). Source: Author's elaboration on EBA (2015b, 2018d). Note: EBA 2015 EU-wide Transparency Exercise does not report aggregate figures on sovereign exposures for banks incorporated in Estonia and Greece at the end of 2013

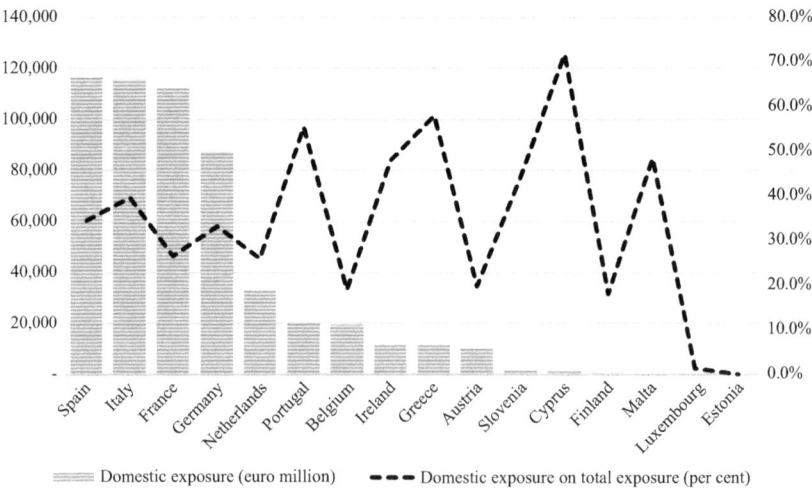

Fig. 4.6   Sovereign debt securities domestic exposure. Source: Author's elaboration on EBA (2018d). Note: Domestic exposure in euro million is reported on the left-hand Y axis. Domestic exposure to total exposure in percentage is reported on the right-hand Y axis. EBA 2018 EU-wide Transparency Exercise does not report aggregate figures on sovereign exposures for banks incorporated in Latvia, Lithuania and Slovakia

4.3.2   Theoretical Explanations

Scholars have recently debated the home bias issue. At least two competing explanations for home bias in sovereign debt can be identified: financial repression by governments or risk-shifting strategies of domestic banks. Financial repression refers to government policies which aim to confer benefits to the government as a borrower at the expense of the lender. Among the proponents of the financial repression hypothesis is Uhlig (2014), who argues that supervisory rules induce banks in countries with weak fiscal fundamentals to purchase domestic bonds and refinance these via repos with a multilateral central bank. Becker and Ivashina (2014) find evidence that direct government ownership and influence via banks' boards of directors are channels used to exercise financial repression. Similarly, Horvath et al. (2015) report evidence that home bias in government bond purchases is higher for banks owned by risky sovereign states. De Marco and Macchiavelli (2016) show that politics is at the root of the banks–sovereign nexus that exacerbated the euro area crisis. Government-owned banks or banks with politicians in the boards of directors naturally display higher home bias in sovereign debt compared to privately owned banks. Nevertheless, only government-owned banks increased the home bias during the sovereign debt crisis, pointing towards a moral suasion explanation. De Marco and Macchiavelli (2016) also proved that moral suasion is stronger in countries under stress. By using a novel dataset on bank-level exposures to sovereign and private debt covering the entire euro area crisis, Saka (2017) confirms the financial repression or moral suasion explanation, as sovereign debt was reallocated from foreign to domestic banks at the peak of the crisis. Similar evidence can be found in Brutti and Sauré (2016).

As for the risk-shifting hypothesis, it implies that a bank purchases government debt to maximise expected returns for bank shareholders; that is, home bias is a voluntary, optimal portfolio choice rather than an investment imposed by government action. Because of limited liability, the pay-off structure of bank portfolio decisions is asymmetric for bank shareholders in the sense that the downside is capped by their participation in the capital of the bank, while the upside is not restricted. Accordingly, risk can be shifted from bank shareholders to bank creditors (Andreeva and Vlassopoulos 2016). Consistent with this view, Horvath et al. (2015) find that home bias in sovereign bond purchases is greater if bank corporate governance regimes are more shareholder friendly. Risk-shifting by undercapitalised banks is among the driving factors of domestic sovereign bond purchases found by Acharya and Steffen (2015). Crosignani (2015) emphasises the interrelationship between undercapitalised banks' investment in domestic sovereign bonds and the willingness of governments to recapitalise banks. Sovereign states with difficult access to financial markets might be unwilling to recapitalise weak (but still solvent) domestic banks so that the latter will continue to act as buyers of last resort of government debt, which they would be less inclined to do if they were well capitalised.

As a matter of fact, domestic sovereign bonds are an important part of banks' portfolios in "normal" times. Historical experience shows that in normal times EU banks autonomously reduced their sovereign portfolios (as well as the concentration) without any significant change in prudential treatment of sovereign exposures (Visco 2015). Indeed, the evidence suggests that most EU countries' sovereign holdings behaved counter-cyclically: they declined during the normal period between the introduction of the euro and the beginning of the financial crisis; increased during the crisis period; and started once more to decline from 2014, as the crisis began to subside. During default years, however, banks with average exposure to government bonds exhibit a lower growth rate of loans than banks without bonds. These results indicate that the "dangerous embrace" between banks and their government plays a key role during sovereign defaults, and its strength depends on local conditions (Gennaioli et al. 2018). Indeed, banks in emerging economies hold a larger amount of bonds in normal times (12.7 per cent of assets in non-OECD [Organisation for Economic Co-operation and Development] countries) as compared to the holdings by banks in developed economies (5 per cent of assets in OECD countries). It is only natural to expect that these normal-times holdings should account for the bulk of the adverse effects of sovereign defaults on bank lending. Local conditions may have significant implications for bank regulation.

4.3.3   Policymakers' Debate

Until the end of 2017, a vivid debate on home bias took place. The possible options ranged from assigning to the domestic sovereign exposures a non-zero risk weight and/or subjecting them to concentration limits, to keeping the framework unchanged. Some policymakers and academics suggest that a general and mandatory (Pillar 1) requirement should focus on sovereign concentration risk rather than sovereign credit risk, constraining only large exposures as opposed to the risk weighting of all sovereign assets (Veron 2017). Because the home bias problem is unique to the euro area, the new requirement should only be binding for the euro area sovereign exposures of euro area banks. A Sovereign Concentration Charges Regulation (SCCR) would add sovereign exposures above a certain threshold (defined as a ratio to Tier 1 capital), weighted by a coefficient (sovereign concentration charge) that increases with the exposure ratio, to risk weighted assets in the capital ratio's denominator. The charges for concentrated sovereign exposures to different euro area countries would add up.

The proposed calibration for the SCCR should be lenient, to avert any risk of disturbance in sovereign debt markets. Sovereign exposures under 33 per cent of Tier 1 capital would be entirely exempted. The marginal capital charges on concentrated exposures would be mild for exposures up to 100 per cent of Tier 1 capital and rise more steeply above that level. Should this calibration turn out to have an insufficient impact, it could be strengthened at a later stage. The calibration suggested by Veron (2017), however, does not take into consideration the interaction of the add-ons with the liquidity requirements—the liquidity coverage ratio (LCR) and the net stable funding ratio (NSFR)—introduced in the aftermath of the financial crisis. Therefore this calibration would not allow banks to meet the LCR by using sovereign bonds, which are the only financial instruments that are very liquid (Lanotte and Tommasino 2018).

Assigning banks' sovereign exposures a non-zero risk weight, under this view, would increase capital and thus the resilience of the banking system. Introducing rules to discourage a high concentration of sovereign exposure would increase banks' chances of surviving a sovereign default, preventing them from playing a shock amplifier role, as in recent cases of distress of sovereign states with weak economic fundamentals. Furthermore, if risk weights accurately reflect sovereign risk, they can incentivise banks' risk management of sovereign exposure by recognising that the higher return from riskier counterparties comes at a cost of increased incurred risk. Also, in case a crowding out of private lending by public debt exists, a risk-sensitive approach for sovereign risk could reduce this effect and promote the more efficient allocation of resources, leading to higher investment and higher potential GDP growth.

As for the second option, that is keeping the framework unchanged, Visco (2015) notes that recent amendments of the regulatory and legal framework have already made substantial progress towards breaking the bank–sovereign loop. In Europe, the banks-to-sovereign causal link has been addressed by bank-related reforms, beginning with the *Bank Recovery and Resolution Directive* (BRRD). On the prudential front, banks' sovereign exposures are taken into consideration in the capital exercise and stress test frameworks applied since the end of 2011—the results of which are nowadays taken into account in the Pillar 2 capital buffers required within the Supervisory Review and Evaluation Process (SREP)—and through the introduction of the leverage ratio. Furthermore, the European fiscal framework has been enhanced across several dimensions, thus addressing the sovereign-to-bank nexus. The Stability and Growth Pact has been amended, reinforcing both its preventive and its corrective arm; member countries have strengthened their national budgetary processes and institutions; and a surveillance mechanism has been set up for early detection and correction of macroeconomic imbalances (Visco 2015). Finally, the European Stability Mechanism was established.

Tightening regulatory standards on domestic sovereign exposures may not be sufficient to safeguard banks against sovereign default. Direct exposures are just one of the channels that transmit sovereign risk to the domestic banking system. Sovereign defaults are associated with severe economic crises, which have a widespread negative impact on domestic banks quite independently from the degree of their direct exposure.

In addition, given that in normal times banks' sovereign exposure declines spontaneously, the imposition of risk weights or tight concentration limits could create substantive difficulties in "crisis" times. These rules could be particularly disruptive for banks' ability to act as shock absorbers in the event of sovereign stress and could serve as a coordinating device for speculative attacks. To the extent that banks sell assets when markets overheat and buy when they are excessively bearish, purchases of sovereign debt when the sovereign state experiences difficulties, notwithstanding relatively solid economic fundamentals, are actually beneficial to financial stability (Visco 2015).

Finally, a system which differentiates the risk weights according to the sovereign state's credit risk could end up relying upon ratings issued by the credit rating agencies. Credit ratings of sovereign states have serious shortcomings, as they tend to be backward looking and foster herd behaviour. As such, they could exacerbate pro-cyclicality and ultimately increase financial instability risk.

Against this background, ESRB (2015) highlights that risks from sovereign exposures come in different forms depending on whether the country in question is a member of the euro area or whether it has its own currency. Because EU legislation applies to all Member States, harmonisation of regulatory rules might be deemed to call for all sovereign exposures to be treated alike. However, such treatment would neglect the specific situation of countries with national currencies other than the euro. Such differences concern not only the risk of sovereign default but also the scope for diversifying risks by investing in debt issued by different sovereign states; for banks in a country with its own currency, any attempt to diversify risks across sovereign states would involve an exchange rate risk. Nevertheless, the preceding views are not shared by some expert group members of ESRB (2015), who argue that, in the context of risks from sovereign exposure, there are no systematic differences between countries with their own currencies and countries in the euro area.

4.3.4 High-Level Task Force on Sovereign Exposures

On top of the debate described above, in January 2015, the Basel Committee on Banking Supervision initiated a review of the existing regulatory treatment of sovereign risk. The committee set up a high-level Task Force on Sovereign Exposures to review the regulatory treatment of sovereign exposures and to recommend potential policy options. Despite the issues raised by the task force and the fact that the potential ideas outlined are important and could benefit from a broader discussion, the committee has not reached a consensus to make any changes to the treatment of sovereign exposures and has therefore decided not to consult on the ideas presented by the task force (BIS 2017).

All sovereign exposures entail risks, but they also play an important role in the banking system, financial markets and the broader economy, as outlined by Visco (2015). Sovereign risk has various dimensions, and the sovereign–bank nexus is multifaceted, potentially serving as an amplifier and/or absorber of shocks in times of crisis. Sovereign exposures play an important and heterogeneous role across different markets and jurisdictions. For instance, sovereign exposures are used by banks for liquidity management, credit risk mitigation, asset pricing, financial intermediation and investment purposes (BIS 2017). Banks' holdings of sovereign exposures also play an important role as part of monetary policy. As banks are generally one of the main investors in government debt, they also play a role in fiscal policy.

The existing treatment of sovereign exposures is more favourable than for other asset classes. The risk-weighted framework includes a national discretion that permits applying a zero per cent risk weight for sovereign exposures denominated and funded in domestic currency, regardless of their inherent risk. This discretion is currently exercised by all members of the committee. Sovereign exposures are also currently exempted from the large exposures framework. Moreover, no limits or haircuts are applied to domestic sovereign exposures that are eligible as high-quality liquid assets. In contrast, sovereign exposures are included as part of the leverage ratio framework.

In addition, BIS (2017) sets out some ideas regarding the regulatory treatment of sovereign exposures. It starts by reviewing the existing perimeter and segmentation of sovereign exposures and presents possible revisions to the definition of sovereign entities to ensure greater consistency across jurisdictions. Among other proposals, it suggests mitigating the risks of excessive holdings of sovereign exposures by introducing increasing marginal add-ons on sovereign exposures exceeding a given set of thresholds, regardless of the nationality (domestic vs. foreign) and the riskiness of the sovereign exposures. This proposal represents an interesting step forward in the debate, but still raises doubts. For instance, as it is meant to apply to euro area banks only, it could seriously skew the level playing field for EU banks with an international reach, especially now that the Basel Committee, after careful consideration, has decided to shelve the issue at the international level (Lanotte and Tommasino 2018).

4.4   Conclusion

In the asset quality review and stress test carried out by the Single Supervisory Mechanism in conjunction with the European Banking Authority, the assets and the underlying modelling assumptions are assessed indirectly and only in a qualitative way. By contrast, the SSM has always placed great emphasis on the assessment of credit risk underlying the portfolios of commercial banks. This skewed approach has been criticised by some banks as evidence of a bias towards banks which are relatively more specialised in wholesale banking over those more oriented towards commercial banking. L3 assets are, nonetheless, a significant source of risk for euro area banks. Despite the relevant amount of these assets held by banks, there is still limited information (accounting, prudential and market data) on L3 assets, and an exhaustive mapping of the actual risk factors is not available for several reasons. First, the liquidity of the relevant markets is generally low; second, the reliability and comparability of the pricing models used by banks are partially unknown; and third, the discretion of the accounting and prudential regulations may further contribute to complexity and opacity of these assets, making it difficult to detect potential mispricing of risk and valuation uncertainties. Prudential authorities are widely aware of risks embedded in L3 assets, which represent a potential obstacle to the completion of the Banking Union.

Addressing the home bias problem can be seen as another step towards stronger euro area integration. Whereas it is ascertained that banks' excessive exposure to domestic sovereign debt may hurt their balance sheets in the time of a crisis, the strategies, if any, to tackle this problem need further discussion.

On top of this, any reform of regulatory rules will have to be addressed by the appropriate decision-making bodies, internationally at the level of the Basel Committee on Banking Supervision (BCBS) and other bodies, and, for legislation and actual supervision, at the level of EU authorities, starting with a legislative proposal from the EC, and at the level of national authorities. It would be important for the regulatory authorities to obtain detailed information and impact assessments which should also consider the long-run impact of different (and/or combinations of) policy measures. Given the sensitivity and the potential impact of any change in regulation, the timing of such deliberations, as well as the timing of the introduction of new measures and the rules for transition, needs to be carefully considered. At a time of crisis, any consideration of new measures imposing burdens on banks and/or making sovereign funding more difficult can have a negative impact on markets, which might exacerbate the crisis. Even if the transition is allowed to take a long time, announcement effects might occur immediately.

In line with BIS (2017), both theory and experience seem to suggest that such a reform would have small net benefits in most states of the world, while it could instead increase tail risks related to the possibility of non-linear investors' reactions and of multiple market equilibria. Close ties between sovereign states and banks are arguably an intrinsic feature of the modern macroeconomy. It might be possible that further changes in prudential regulation are not the right instrument for addressing the sovereign–bank nexus, taking into account that sovereign risk should first and foremost be addressed by strengthening the sustainability of public finance (Visco 2015; Lanotte and Tommasino 2018).

NOTES

1. Fair value measurement of financial instruments is addressed by IFRS 13.
2. Examples of L2 directly observable inputs include quoted prices for similar instruments in both active and not active markets; examples of L2 indirectly observable inputs include interest rates, implied volatilities and credit spreads that are derived from quoted prices (e.g. bonds, options and credit default swaps). Examples of L3 inputs include financial forecasts of cash flows or profits used in a present value technique, long-term volatilities and correlations, recovery rates and nonlisted counterparty credit risk (Banca d'Italia 2017).
3. For example, two otherwise identical plain vanilla swaps may be L2 or L3 depending on the observability of the counterparty credit risk.
4. The sample covers all euro area banks with total assets larger than 30 billion in 2017 on Orbis Bank. It includes significant institutions as classified by the European Central Bank.
5. The EBA sample is different from the sample downloaded from Orbis Bank in several aspects: the Orbis Bank sample reports data on a sample of 119 large euro area banks; the EBA sample covers a list of banks which includes global systemically important institutions (G-SII) and also other large institutions with an overall exposure measure of more than 200 billion euro and which are potentially systemically relevant. These 36 banks should provide data which contribute to assess EU banks' systemic riskiness following the EBA Guidelines on disclosure of indicators of global systemic importance and the Basel Committee recommendations and efforts to identify global systemically important banks (EBA 2016; BIS 2018).
6. A comprehensive description of the topic is provided by Banca d'Italia (2017).

REFERENCES

Acharya, V., and S. Steffen. 2015. The greatest carry trade ever? Understanding Eurozone bank risks. *Journal of Financial Economics* 112 (2): 215–236.
Andreeva, D.C., and T. Vlassopoulos. 2016. *Home bias in bank sovereign bond purchases and the bank-sovereign nexus.* ECB Working Paper 1977, November.
Andritzky, J., N. Gadatsch, T. Körner, A. Schäfer, and I. Schnabel. 2016. *A proposal for ending the privileges for sovereign exposures in banking regulation.* VoxEU.org, March 4.
Banca D'italia. 2017. Risks and challenges of complex financial instruments: An analysis of SSM banks. *Questioni di Economia e Finanza*, Occasional Papers, no. 417, December 2017.

Becker, B., and V. Ivashina. 2014. *Financial repression in the European sovereign debt crisis.* http://ssrn.com/abstract=2429767.

BIS. 2017. *The regulatory treatment of sovereign exposures.* Discussion Paper, December.

———. 2018. *Global systemically important banks: Revised assessment methodology and the higher loss absorbency requirement*, July.

———. 2019a. *Instructions for the End-2018 G-SIB assessment exercise*, January.

———. 2019b. *Minimum capital requirements for market risk*, January (rev. February).

———. 2019c. *Explanatory note on the minimum capital requirements for market risk.*

Brutti, F., and P. Sauré. 2016. Repatriation of debt in the euro crisis. *Journal of the European Economic Association* 14: 145–174.

Crosignani, M. 2015. *Why are banks not recapitalized during crises?* Oesterreichische Nationalbank Working Paper 203.

De Marco F., and M. Macchiavelli. 2016. *The political origin of home bias: The case of Europe.* Finance and Economics Discussion Series 2016-060. Washington, DC: Board of Governors of the Federal Reserve System. https://doi.org/10.17016/FEDS.2016.060.

EBA. 2015a. *EBA final draft regulatory technical standards on prudent valuation under article 105(14) of regulation* (EU). No 575/2013 (Capital Requirements Regulation—CRR), EBA/RTS/2014/06/rev1, January.

———. 2015b. 2015 EU-wide transparency exercise. https://eba.europa.eu/risk-analysis-and-data/eu-wide-transparency-exercise/2015/results.

———. 2016. *Final guidelines revised guidelines on the further specification of the indicators of global systemic importance and their disclosure.* EBA/GL/2016/01, February.

———. 2018a. *2018 EU-wide stress test methodological note*, January.

———. 2018b. *2018 EU-wide stress test results*, November.

———. 2018c. *Large institutions with a leverage ratio exposure measure above 200bn.* EUR, interactive tool. https://eba.europa.eu/risk-analysis-and-data/global-systemically-important-institutions/2018.

———. 2018d. 2018 EU-wide transparency exercise results. https://eba.europa.eu/risk-analysis-and-data/eu-wide-transparency-exercise/2018/results.

ECB. 2014. *Asset quality review, phase 2.* Manual, March.

ESRB. 2015. *Report on the regulatory treatment of sovereign exposures*, March.

Gennaioli, N., A. Martin, and S. Rossi. 2014. Sovereign default, domestic banks, and financial institutions. *Journal of Finance* 69: 819–866.

———. 2018. Banks, government bonds, and default: What do the data say? *Journal of Monetary Economics* 98: 1–16.

Horvath, B., H. Huizinga, and V. Ioannidou. 2015. *Determinants and valuation effects of the home bias in European banks' sovereign debt portfolios.* CEPR Discussion Paper Series, No. 10661.

Korte, J., and S. Steffen. 2014. *A 'sovereign subsidy': Zero risk weights and sovereign risk spillovers.* VoxEU.org, September 7.

Lanotte, M., and P. Tommasino. 2018. *Recent developments in the regulatory treatment of sovereign exposures.* VoxEU.org, February 5.

Saka, O. 2017. *Domestic banks as lightning rods? Home bias during the Eurozone crisis.* LSE 'Europe in Question' Discussion Paper Series, LEQS Paper No. 122/2017, February.

Sironi, A. 2018. *The evolution of banking regulation since the financial crisis: A critical assessment.* Baffi Carefin Centre Research Paper No. 2018-103.

Uhlig, H. 2014. Sovereign default risk and banks in a monetary union. *German Economic Review* 15 (1): 23–41.

Veron, N. 2017. *Sovereign concentration charges: A new regime for banks' sovereign exposures.* Bruegel and Peterson Institute for International Economics, November.

Visco, I. 2015. *The future of European government bonds markets banks' sovereign exposures and the feedback loop between banks and their sovereigns.* Concluding Remarks, Euro50 Group Meeting, Banca d'Italia.

CHAPTER 5

Progress on the First Two Pillars of the Banking Union

5.1 Introduction

After the global financial crisis, the institutional and regulatory framework for European banks has been fundamentally reinforced, resulting in a substantial reduction of risks in the banking sector. Several key elements of the Banking Union are already established. First, the Single Rulebook provides a unique set of harmonised prudential rules that banks must respect in the Single Market. The Banking Union works on this basis, which applies in all Member States. Second, all banks in the European Union are supervised according to the same standards, with the most significant banks in the euro area being centrally supervised by the European Central Bank in the framework of the Single Supervisory Mechanism (SSM). Third, in the case of failure, banks can be resolved centrally and according to the same standards within the Single Resolution Mechanism (SRM), which is backed by a Single Resolution Fund (SRF). The establishment of this new architecture for the Banking Union has been accompanied by a comprehensive asset quality review, stress test and recapitalisation exercises for participating banks since 2014.

The first review of the SSM by the European Commission shows that the establishment of the Single Supervisory Mechanism was overall successful (EC 2017a).

In addition, the Single Resolution Mechanism has managed its first bank resolution case, with no cost for taxpayers.[1] This shows that the new

© The Author(s) 2019
F. Arnaboldi, *Risk and Regulation in Euro Area Banks*, Palgrave Macmillan Studies in Banking and Financial Institutions,
https://doi.org/10.1007/978-3-030-23429-4_5

system is able to manage a bank resolution efficiently and in a very short period of time, while at the same time allowing for different crisis management options, as provided for in the legal framework. This allows the specific situation of individual banks to be taken into account, which is particularly important given that there are still significant legacy issues in parts of the European Union banking sector and not all elements of the Banking Union are fully operational (EC 2017b).

While several improvements can be made in the short term, other issues can only be tackled fully once the Banking Union is completed. In this context, this chapter focuses on the progress achieved and rules to be completed on the first and second pillar of the Banking Union. Chapter 6 will then examine another missing piece, that is, the single European Deposit Insurance Scheme (EDIS).

5.2   REVISED RULES ON CAPITAL REQUIREMENTS AND RESOLUTION

The EU has implemented a substantial financial-sector reform agenda in recent years. In this context, the regulatory framework for banks has been strengthened on the basis of common rules, which ensure more consistent regulation and high-quality supervision across the EU. This framework comprises, in principle, stronger prudential requirements for banks, based on new global standards, introduced under the Capital Requirements Directive (2013/36/EU; CRD IV) and the Capital Requirements Regulation (575/2013; CRR), which transpose into the EU the new Basel III global standards on bank capital. Although the new EU rules entered into force in 2013, they have only been fully applied since 1 January 2019. The aim of CRD IV and CRR is to enhance the capacity of banks to absorb adverse economic and financial shocks by increasing the quality and quantity of capital, expanding risk coverage, containing leverage and improving governance and transparency.

In addition, a new recovery and resolution framework for banks that are failing or likely to fail has been established under the Bank Recovery and Resolution Directive (2014/59/EU; BRRD). This framework allows Member States to manage bank crises in a more timely and orderly manner, with the goal of avoiding use of taxpayers' money.

A key objective of the Banking Union is to reverse the fragmentation of financial markets since the euro crisis, by weakening the link between banks and their national sovereigns as bank failures can endanger public finances, and sovereign stress can affect banks. In order to meet this objective, it was decided that the supervision, resolution and resolution funding of significant banks should be conducted at the Banking Union level. To this end, the Single Supervisory Mechanism (SSM) and the Single Resolution Mechanism (SRM)—the first two pillars of the Banking Union—have been established. The SSM became operational in November 2014 and is in charge of independent and uniform prudential supervision. The SRM, which defined the rules on the recovery and resolution of failing institutions and established the Single Resolution Mechanism, became fully operational in January 2016, when contributions to the Single Resolution Fund (SRF) began.

In addition to these progresses, European regulators employ a parallel effort to further reduce risks in the banking sector and weaken the link between banks and their national sovereign. The rules and regulations on NPLs, Level 3 assets and sovereign exposures, examined in the previous chapters, all move in this direction.

Even if the work on the first two pillars of the Banking Union has significantly progressed, a number of initiatives with the aim of further reducing risk and improving risk management in banks continue (Table 5.1).

Table 5.1 Completing the Banking Union (BU): milestones

22 June 2015	Five Presidents' Report
24 November 2015	EDIS proposal
24 November 2015	Communication towards the completion of the BU
17 June 2016	Council roadmap to complete the BU
4 November 2016	Draft EP report on EDIS
22 November 2016	Business insolvency proposal
23 November 2016	Commission's Banking Package
31 May 2017	Reflection paper on the deepening of the EMU
11 October 2017	Communication on completing the BU
29 November 2017	Commission's stock take on risk-reduction measures
6 December 2017	EMU package (including a proposal on the establishment of a EMF)
14 March 2018	NPL legislative package
24 May 2018	Framework for Sovereign Bond-Backed Securities proposed by Commission
14 December 2018	Euro Summit agreement on SRF Backstop, on setting up a High-Level Expert Group to continue work on EDIS and on further work on liquidity in resolution
7 June 2019	Banking Package—CRD V CRR II

Source: Author's elaboration on EP (2019a)

5.2.1   2016 Commission Package

In November 2016, the Commission presented a review of the prudential framework under the name of the CRD V package, comprising a proposal for a regulation amending the CRR and a proposal for a directive amending the CRD IV (EC 2016a, b). The proposal aimed to complete the reform agenda by also amending the BRRD and the Single Resolution Mechanism Regulation (806/2014; SRMR).

The Commission proposal incorporates the remaining elements of the regulatory framework agreed within the Basel Committee on Banking Supervision (BCBS) and the Financial Stability Board (FSB) to increase the resilience of EU institutions and enhance financial stability, such as, more risk-sensitive capital requirements, in particular in the area of market risk, counterparty credit risk and for exposures to central counterparties (CCPs); implementing methodologies that are able to reflect more accurately the actual risks to which banks are exposed; a binding leverage ratio (LR) to prevent institutions from excessive leverage; a binding Net Stable Funding Ratio (NSFR) to address the excessive reliance on short-term wholesale funding and to reduce long-term funding risk; a requirement for global systemically important institutions (G-SIIs) to hold minimum levels of capital and other instruments, which bear losses in resolution (Total Loss-Absorbing Capacity or TLAC). The TLAC is integrated into the existing Minimum Requirement for own funds and Eligible Liabilities (MREL) system, which is applicable to all banks, to strengthen the EU's ability to resolve failing G-SIIs while protecting financial stability and minimising risks for taxpayers.

The proposal also included measures to improve banks' lending capacity to support the EU economy, such as the introduction of CRD/CRR rules that are more proportionate and less burdensome for smaller and less complex banks where some of the current disclosure, reporting and complex trading book-related requirements appear not to be justified by prudential considerations, and to further facilitate the role of banks in achieving greater and more liquid EU capital markets to support the creation of a Capital Markets Union.

These legislative proposals have been finally adopted in 2019 by the European Parliament and the Council after intense negotiations (EP 2019b, c).

5.2.2   Directive (EU) 2019/878 (CRD V) and Regulation (EU) 2019/876 (CRR II)

The CRD V, which has to be transposed by Member States by December 2020, and Regulation EU 2019/876, which applies from June 2021 (the "banking package"), aim to address issues raised in relation to the provisions of Directive 2013/36/EU, which proved not to be sufficiently clear and have therefore been subject to divergent interpretations or which have been found to be too onerous for certain banks. It also contains adjustments to Directive 2013/36/EU that are necessary following either the adoption of other relevant Union legal acts, such as Directive 2014/59/EU of the European Parliament and of the Council, or the changes proposed in parallel to Regulation (EU) 575/2013. Finally, the amendments proposed better align the current regulatory framework to international developments in order to promote consistency and comparability among jurisdictions. The banking package specifically addresses two topics: capital and liquidity requirements and bank crisis management framework.

5.2.2.1 Capital and Liquidity Requirements

As for the capital and liquidity requirements, a binding leverage ratio (LR) requirement, which is a capital requirement independent from the riskiness of the exposures, as a backstop to risk-weighted capital requirements, is introduced for all banks subject to the CRR. The LR requirement is set at 3 per cent of Tier 1 capital and banks must meet this in addition to/in parallel with their risk-based capital requirements. The 3 per cent calibration is in line with the internationally agreed level and, according to the European Parliament, the Council and the European Commission, would constitute a credible backstop function. G-SIIs are set to hold an additional leverage ratio buffer on top of the leverage ratio applicable to all banks. This additional requirement was not included in the 2016 Commission's proposal, but it has been added in the package during the negotiations between the European Parliament and the Council (EC 2019b).

Liquidity requirements include the NSFR, which aims to ensure that exposures are matched with stable funding sources, thus preventing liquidity crises. The NSFR standard agreed by the Basel Committee is implemented with some adjustments recommended by the EBA (2015). They relate mainly to specific treatments such as pass-through models in general and covered bonds issuance in particular, whose funding risk can be considered as low when assets and liabilities have the same maturity. The proposed specific treatments broadly reflect the preferential treatment granted to these activities in the EU liquidity coverage ratio (LCR). As the NSFR complements the LCR, these two ratios need to be consistent in their definition and calibration (EP 2019b).

A compromise has also been reached on market risk capital requirements. Since the level of capital required against trading book positions proved insufficient to absorb losses when they materialised during the financial crisis, BIS (2013) carried out a fundamental review of the trading book (FRTB) framework. The FRTB standard of the Basel Committee as a whole was completed in January 2016. However, certain elements of the new market risk framework were subsequently revised by the Basel Committee in January 2019.[2] In light of these developments, which came after the Commission's proposal, the European Parliament and the Council agreed that it would not be appropriate to implement the FRTB rules as initially proposed by the Commission because it would force banks to meet requirements subject to change in the short term. Instead, the legislators have adopted a reporting requirement. Reporting will start once the elements reviewed at international level are introduced via a delegated act for the standardised approach and via technical standards developed by the EBA for the internal model approach (EC 2019b). The EBA has been mandated to report to the Commission on the appropriateness of the final FRTB standards for capital requirement purposes and, in light of this report, the Commission will be invited to submit a legislative proposal by June 2020 to turn the reporting requirement based on the FRTB approaches into a capital requirement.

The banking package also addresses the treatment of software assets. As a general rule, banks are required to deduct the value of software assets identified as intangible from their capital. This rule increases their capital needs and potentially reduces investments in software. The banking business is, however, facing a digital evolution, which can be supported by legislators by allowing banks not to deduct certain types of software assets from own funds. This specification of deductible software is important as software is a broad concept that covers many different types of assets, not all of which preserve their value in a winding-down situation. The EBA will draft technical standards to identify the deductible software assets to ensure prudential soundness, taking into account the difference in accounting rules at international level as well as the diversity of the EU financial sector including fintech.

In addition, the banking package clarifies the conditions for the application of Pillar 2 capital add-ons and the distinction between mandatory

Pillar 2 requirements and supervisory expectations to hold additional capital, also known as Pillar 2 Guidance. Furthermore, it confirms that Pillar 2 capital add-ons should be confined to a purely microprudential perspective to avoid overlaps with the existing macroprudential tools, which aim to address systemic risk. On a similar note, the macroprudential toolbox flexibility and comprehensiveness have been reinforced, for instance by increasing the authorities' flexibility in the use of the Systemic Risk Buffer and the Other Systemically Important Institutions Buffer; by reducing the administrative burden linked to the activation and reciprocation of macroprudential instruments; and by reflecting progress with respect to the Banking Union in the calculation of the G-SII score.

As far as credit risk is concerned, the adopted text includes amendments to the existing credit risk framework in two areas: (1) provisions that would help banks with high levels of NPLs to sell them with a limited impact on their capital requirements (so-called massive disposals) and (2) a more favourable treatment for pensions and salary-backed loans. Banks usually sell large parts of a portfolio of non-performing loans as part of a multiple-year programme and have the objective of reducing non-performing exposure on their balance sheet. When selling, though, banks generally realise losses as massive disposals may not reflect the true long-term economic value of the underlying loans. These losses are one of the parameters used by internal models to estimate loss given default (LGD), thus massive disposals could lead to an unjustified increase in banks' loss estimates and subsequently to higher capital requirements. The new rules allow banks to adjust their loss estimates for a limited period and under strict conditions. This should make it easier for banks to clean up their balance sheets from NPLs.

In terms of proportionality, for smaller and less complex banks the banking package simplifies disclosure requirement and, where new prudential standards are introduced, proposes simple and conservative alternatives, in particular for market risk, the NSFR, counterparty credit risk and interest rate risk in the banking book.

The banking package also affects the financing of small and medium enterprises (SMEs) and infrastructure investment and sustainable finance. With regard to lending to SMEs, the banking package raises the threshold below which exposures to SMEs can benefit from the existing 25 per cent reduction in capital requirements for lending to SMEs. Compared to the existing rules, it also reduces capital requirements by 15 per cent for exposures above that threshold. Similarly, to the prudential requirements on insurance, the banking package lowers capital requirements by 25 per cent for investments in infrastructure provided they comply with a set of criteria able to reduce their risk profile and enhance predictability of cash flows. As for sustainable finance, the European Banking Authority has drafted a report on how to incorporate environmental, social and governance (ESG) risks into the supervisory process and a second document on the prudential treatment of assets associated with environmental or social objectives. In addition, the banking package requires large banks to publicly disclose information on ESG-related risks they are exposed to.

The agreement, likely in the light of Brexit, requires third-country groups with significant EU activities of at least 40 euro billions, regardless of whether they are G-SIIs or not, to set up an intermediate parent undertaking (IPU) in the EU, which would allow for a better supervision of the EU activities and would facilitate resolution within the EU (EC 2019b).

The banking package also introduces amendments to improve cooperation between competent authorities on anti-money laundering (AML) activities. In particular, it comprises cooperation and exchange of information requirements between prudential supervisors, anti-money laundering authorities and financial intelligence units (FIUs). The package stipulates that the application of a banking licence must include a description of the arrangements, processes and mechanisms to manage AML and terrorist financing risks. Additionally, the AML dimension is considered in the SREP, including a notification to the EBA and the AML authorities when weaknesses in the governance model, business activities or business model are identified. Along this line, in September 2018, in the wake of several cases of money-laundering in European banks that have occurred despite efforts to strengthen the AML framework through the adoption of the 4th and 5th Anti-Money Laundering Directives (AMLD), the European Commission published an amended proposal to centralise the tasks relating to the prevention of money-laundering and terrorist financing into the EBA (EC 2018).[3] The amended proposal extends the supervisory powers of the EBA related to AML/CFT from the banking sector to the financial sector as a whole, thereby taking over the supervisory powers currently held by ESMA (European Securities and Markets Authority) and EIOPA (European Insurance and Occupational Pensions Authority).

5.2.2.2 Bank Crisis Management Framework

As for the second topic, that is the bank crisis management framework, the most relevant change is on the MREL. In order to ensure effective and credible application of the bail-in resolution tool to impose losses on banks' creditors in case of a banking crisis, banks are subject to the MREL, which was first introduced by Directive 2014/59/EU. The main goal is to avoid that institutions excessively rely on forms of funding that are excluded from bail-in, since failure to meet MREL would impact negatively on banks' loss absorption and recapitalisation capacity and, ultimately, the overall effectiveness of the resolution. In order to achieve a credible bail-in tool, the banking package tightens the rules on the subordination of MREL instruments (EC 2019b). On top of the existing global systemically important banks category, the European Parliament and the Council decided to create a new category of large banks, the so-called top-tier banks with a balance sheet size greater than 100 billion euro, in relation to which more prudent subordination requirements are formulated. National resolution authorities may also select other banks (non-GSIIs, non-top tier banks) and subject them to the top-tier bank treatment. The package creates an MREL minimum Pillar 1 subordination policy for each of these different categories. Moreover, for a subset of G-SIIs and top-tier banks and under certain conditions, the resolution authority may also impose an additional Pillar 2 subordination requirement. In addition, if banks breach their MREL requirements, they may be subject to restrictions preventing them from distributing resources to shareholders or employees.

The enhanced MREL complements the Total Loss-Absorbing Capacity (TLAC) standard introduced in 2015 by the Financial Stability Board for global systemically important banks (FSB 2015). The TLAC standard has been designed with the aim that failing global significant banks will have sufficient loss-absorbing and recapitalisation capacity available in resolution for authorities to implement an orderly resolution that minimises impacts on financial stability, maintains the continuity of critical functions and avoids exposing public funds to loss. The TLAC standard defines a minimum requirement for the instruments and liabilities that should be readily available for bail-in within resolution at global significant banks, but does not limit authorities' powers under the applicable resolution law to expose other liabilities to loss through bail-in or the application of other resolution tools. Those banks are required to meet a minimum TLAC requirement of at least 16 per cent of the resolution group's risk weighted assets (TLAC RWA Minimum) as from 1 January 2019 and at least 18 per cent as from 1 January 2022. Minimum TLAC must also be at least 6 per cent of the Basel III leverage ratio denominator (TLAC Leverage Ratio Exposure [LRE] Minimum) as from 1 January 2019 and at least 6.75 per cent as from 1 January 2022.

The regulation concerning TLAC and MREL impose banks to issue subordinated liabilities that can then be bailed in the case of a bank crisis.

Table 5.2   Key elements of the banking package

A binding 3% leverage ratio
A binding NSFR which will require financial institutions to finance their long-term activities with stable sources of funding
Higher more risk-sensitive capital requirements for institutions that trade in securities and derivatives, following the Basel fundamental review of the trading book
More proportionate rules for smaller and non-complex banks
Rules facilitating lending to SMEs and funding infrastructure projects
Clarified conditions for the application of Pillar 2 capital add-ons

Source: Author's elaboration on EP (2019b, c)

The cost of these additional funds can vary in a significant way across countries and create competitive biases. Potential differences in the costs of funding for large banking groups operating in different countries can significantly affect the level playing field (Sironi 2018).

Furthermore, in order to avoid excessive outflows of liquidity in a bank resolution, it has been agreed to provide a moratorium power, which should be triggered after the bank is declared "failing or likely to fail". This power allows supervisors to impose a moratorium also on covered deposits for a maximum duration of two days. Table 5.2 exhibits the key elements of the banking package.

5.3   WHAT IS LEFT?

5.3.1   Common Backstop

The Banking Union still lacks an effective common backstop. The creation of such a backstop for the Single Resolution Fund was already agreed by Member States in 2013. It needs to be made operational so as to reinforce the overall credibility of the bank resolution framework within the Banking Union. It is essential that actions taken by the Single Resolution Board (SRB) enjoy the absolute confidence of all parties concerned if the key objectives of resolution in terms of maintaining financial stability and minimising costs to taxpayers are to be fully achieved. Together with the application of other resolution tools, that is bail-in, and availability of the SRF, access to a last-resort common backstop should serve to provide such confidence. This would include, for example, using common funding in combination with the European Central Bank instruments to cover liquidity shortfalls and have more time to look for the best buyer of a bank in a specific situation.

On 6 December 2017, the European Commission published a road-map on further steps towards completing the Economic and Monetary Union, including a proposal for a Council Regulation on the establishment of a European Monetary Fund. According to that proposal, the European Monetary Fund (EMF) should act as a backstop for the SRF in case the latter's immediately available resources for capital or liquidity purposes are depleted. The backstop in the form of a credit line or guarantees to the SRF would be fiscally neutral over time, since any funds used would be recovered from the banking sectors in the Member States participating in the Banking Union. EC (2017c) specifically sets out that the provision of credit lines and guarantees to the SRB would be a totally new function for the European Stability Mechanism in comparison to the ESM's current objective and tasks. The combined amount of outstanding commitments for backstopping the SRF shall be subject to a ceiling of 60 billion euro, which could be increased.

On the basis of the EC Communication, the Eurogroup further developed the main elements of an ESM credit line to backstop the SRF. The contours of such a backstop were outlined in the Eurogroup President's 25 June 2018 letter to the President of the European Council. On the 4 December 2018, Eurogroup agreed on terms of reference detailing the main elements of the SRF backstop. The terms of reference conditions' early introduction of the backstop to make sufficient progress in risk-reduction by 2020 "to be assessed with the aim of 5 per cent of gross NPLs and 2.5 per cent net NPL on all banks in the Banking Union, and on adequate build-up of bail-inable liabilities". The 14 December Euro Summit endorsed the terms of reference and mandated Eurogroup to finalise the necessary ESM Treaty amendments by mid-2019 (Table 5.3).

The goal of backstops is to create confidence that bank resolution can always be enacted efficiently, which has a stabilising effect in a crisis and prevents bank contagion. Draghi (2018) highlighted that a good example of this is the Federal Deposit Insurance Corporation (FDIC) in the United States, which is also the resolution authority and is backstopped by a credit line with the US Treasury. During the crisis, nearly 500 banks were resolved in the United States without triggering financial instability. An orderly resolution of this magnitude was possible because of confidence in a well-functioning resolution framework, with the presence of the Treasury backstop being fundamental in creating this confidence. Although the FDIC did not have to draw on its credit line, it was clearly reassuring to markets and to depositors that it had that option as a last resort. With the

Table 5.3 Terms of reference selected elements for the common backstop to the SRF

General characteristics	• The ESM will provide the common backstop, in the form of a revolving credit line. The size of the credit line will be aligned with the target level of the SRF; nominal cap to be set above the initial size and decided by the ESM Board of Governors at the latest at the time of ESM Treaty change; nominal cap can be adjusted by ESM Board of Governors • During the transition period, the size of the backstop will increase each year to remain aligned with that of the SRF • The Direct Recapitalisation Instrument be should be replaced by the common backstop • Regular review of the instrument each 3 years and comprehensive review after 10 years the backstop
Use of the backstop Modalities	• Backstop to cover all possible uses of the SRF, according with the current regulation, subject to adequate safeguards to be discussed in 2019 • Fiscal neutrality (margin of 35 bp in the initial 3 years, step up margin of additional 15 bp after 3 years) • Maturities: 3 years+ possible 2 years extension, with possible upfront 5 years if SRB considers financial stability risks exist (to be decided by the ESM Board of Directors) • Equivalent treatment would be ensured with non-euro area Member States participating in the Banking Union, via parallel credit lines to the SRF
Decision-making arrangements	• ESM BoD could take decisions on the use of the common backstop, arrangements with procedures in place for swift and efficient decision-making (maximum 12 hours after SRB request, extendable to 24 hours; conditional decision to be made by Directors on the basis of all available information; ESM Executive Director may be given time-limited delegation) whilst respecting national constitutional requirements • Backstop Committee and sub-committee to be set up to ensure sharing of information and timely coordination with non-euro area Member States • Representatives of non-euro area Member States participate as observers in Board of Governors' and Directors' meetings dealing with backstop usage • Eurogroup to endeavour finding an agreement on an emergency voting procedure, whilst respecting national constitutional requirements
Early introduction	• Common Backstop would enter into force ahead of 2024 if sufficient progress is achieved in risk-reduction measures, to be assessed by 2020. Political decision against the aim of 5% gross NPLs and 2.5% of net NPLs or adequate provisioning for all SRB banks and progress thereto; build-up of subordinated bail-in buffers in line with 2024 and 2022 targets • Technical work, including on a limited revision of the IGA, to continue

Source: EP (2019a)

right policy framework, risk-reduction and risk-sharing goals are mutually reinforcing. Public risk-sharing through backstops helps reduce risks across the system by containing market panics when a crisis hits. And a strong resolution framework ensures that, when bank failures do happen, very little public risk-sharing is actually needed as the costs are fully borne by the private sector (Draghi 2018).

5.3.2   Capital Markets Union

In parallel to the Banking Union, European legislators started to work on an integrated single European capital market. As Lagarde (2019) recalls, in the United States, the corporate bond market accounts for more than two-fifths of GDP, compared with only one-tenth in the euro area.

The Capital Markets Union (CMU), like the Banking Union, is ultimately about broadening the range of domestic and cross-border financing options for firms and households, who currently store 40 per cent of their financial assets as bank deposits. This leaves them very exposed to the banking sector. As long as this is the case, Europe will be overly reliant on banks for savings instruments and investment financing. Not only would an integrated capital market across the EU help companies and households reduce their reliance on banks, it would also make the system more *resilient* to shocks. It would help achieve a more *uniform* cost of funding for firms across countries.

The CMU's main challenges and opportunities have been drafted by the Commission's Green Paper in 2015 (EC 2015). Obstacles to the integration and development of EU capital markets mainly originate in historical, cultural, economic and legal factors, some of which are deep-rooted and difficult to overcome. These include, for example, the historical preference by business for certain means of financing, the characteristics of pension provision, the application of prudential regulations and administrative hurdles, aspects of corporate governance and company law, data gaps and features of many tax systems, as well as inefficient market structures (EC 2015). Challenges lay, in particular, in three key areas. The first area relates to improving access to finance, including to risk capital, for small and medium enterprises (SMEs) by overcoming information problems, the fragmentation of key market segments and lowering the costs of access to capital markets. Second, the development of the CMU depends on the flow of funds into capital market instruments. Boosting the flow of institutional and retail investment into capital markets would promote the diversification of funding sources. Growing occupational and private pension provision in Europe could result in an increased flow of funds into a more diverse range of investment needs through capital market instruments and facilitate a move towards market-based financing. Enhancing the confidence of retail investors in capital markets and financial intermediaries could also increase the flow of household savings into capital market instruments. A third challenge relates to the barriers that are fragmenting markets and holding back the development of specific market segments. More integrated capital markets, especially for equity, would enhance the shock-absorption capacity of the European economy and allow more investment without increasing levels of indebtedness (EC 2015).

Following the Green Book, in September 2015 the European Commission adopted an action plan setting out a list of over 30 actions and related measures to establish the building blocks of an integrated capital market around three mutually reinforcing dimensions: the EU Single Market, clear and proportionate rules and efficient supervision. The action plan was updated and complemented in June 2017. The programme proposed by the Commission includes 13 legislative proposals that represent the key building blocks of the Capital Markets Union. In addition, the Commission has proposed three legislative proposals to enable the financial sector of the Union to lead the way to a greener and cleaner economy. The Commission has also proposed a number of other non-legislative measures to strengthen capital markets and make them more resilient.

In its communication of March 2019, the European Commission reported on the progress of the CMU (EC 2019a). The Commission has proposed six legislative measures to introduce new EU-wide rules for products, labels and passports. The European Parliament and the Council have adopted or reached a political agreement on five proposals. The Regulations on European venture capital and social entrepreneurship funds, adopted in October 2017, aim to boost investment into venture capital and social projects. They will make it easier for investors to invest in innovative small- and medium-sized companies by opening up the regulation to fund managers of all sizes and by expanding the range of companies that can be invested in. The regulation harmonising the securitisation legal framework and creating simple, transparent and standardised (STS) securitisations, adopted in December 2017, helps to build confidence in the securitisation market, prevent mistakes from the past from reoccurring and free up the balance sheets of banks. A set of regulatory and implementing technical standards are being developed to specify the details of the revamped securitisation framework and ensure its clarity and consistent application in order to achieve the policy goals. In addition to the Securitisation Regulation, the prudential framework for banks and insurers has been amended in order to establish a closer link between the riskiness of a securitisation position and the regulatory capital required. The Regulation on a Pan-European Personal Pension Product, on which a political agreement was reached in December 2018, and then approved in European Parliament's April 2019 plenary session, introduces an EU-wide voluntary pension product that could complement national statutory and occupational pensions. It will give citizens more choice when saving for retirement and help address the demographic challenges of ageing populations by complementing state-based and occupational pensions. In February 2019 a political agreement was reached on common rules on covered bonds. The harmonised rules, based on national high standards and best practice, will contribute to developing covered bonds as a stable and cost-effective source of funding for EU banks. By doing so, they will expand the capacity of banks to provide financing to the real economy. They will also give investors a wider range of safer investment opportunities. In February 2019, agreement was also reached on the package on facilitating cross-border distribution of collective investment funds. The new rules will make the cross-border distribution of funds simpler, quicker and cheaper. They will do so by improving the transparency of national requirements, cutting red tape and harmonising diverging national rules. This will provide investors with more choice, and reduce their costs, while safeguarding investor protection. Finally, the proposals for a regulation on crowdfunding, still under negotiation, would allow platforms to apply for an EU licence based on a single set of rules and would therefore make it possible for crowdfunding platforms to provide their services across the EU. The framework would improve access to an innovative form of finance for businesses in need of funding—start-ups in particular—while ensuring that investors benefit from strong protection measures.

While the Commission's action has already started to have an effect, it will take some time for the full impact to be realised and the Capital Markets Union to fully complement the Banking Union. However, more work is clearly needed and, eventually, future action should reflect the impact on capital markets of the United Kingdom's departure from the EU and other short- or medium-term economic and societal challenges.

5.4   CONCLUSION

It Has long been understood that deeper financial integration would lead to a better functioning of the Economic and Monetary Union. Single European supervision and resolution frameworks have, overall, proved beneficial to the banking industry. Risk assessments have become more harmonised and systematic, whereas in the past, broad discretion in applying EU rules led to significant national differences in key prudential aspects, such as the definition of funds, or capital and liquidity requirements. Despite having a single supervisor and more harmonised rules, the banking market in Europe remains fragmented. There are fundamental legal, judicial, political and cultural differences among countries, which are obstacles to cross-border integration. To create a stronger Economic and Monetary Union several actions should still be taken. For instance, the proposals on the development of secondary markets for non-performing loans and an enabling framework for the development of EU sovereign bond-backed securities, currently under discussion, would help complete the Banking Union. The third Pillar of the Banking Union is still under discussion, as is investigated in the next chapter.

NOTES

1. Banco Popular Español was resolved after the positive result of the Public Interest Assessment (PIA). On June 2017, Banco Santander acquired 100 per cent of the share capital of Banco Popular Español as a result of a competitive sale process organised in the framework of a resolution scheme adopted by the Single Resolution Board. As part of the execution of the resolution scheme, all the shares of Banco Popular outstanding at the closing of market on 6 June 2017, and all the shares resulting from the conversion of the regulatory capital instruments Additional Tier 1 issued by Banco Popular, have been totally cancelled and all the regulatory capital instruments Tier 2 issued by Banco Popular have been converted into newly issued shares of Banco Popular, all of which have been acquired for a price of one euro (€1). Moreover, as part of the transaction, on July 2017, Banco Santander carried out a share capital increase of 7072 million to cover the capital and the provisions required to reinforce the balance sheet of Banco Popular. The shareholders of Banco Santander had preferential subscription rights in the share capital increase. Banco Santander holds underwriting commitments for the total of such amount (Santander 2017).
2. In December 2017, the Basel Committee also announced a delay of the implementation deadline of the FRTB standard to 1 January 2022 (BIS 2017).

3. Danske Bank, Denmark's biggest bank, has admitted to having handled through its Estonian branch 200 billion euros of suspicious transactions between 2007 and 2015. Deutsche Bank had to pay a fine of US $425 million in 2017 in the United States over a "mirror trading" scheme that moved US $10 billion out of Russia between 2011 and 2015. Societe Generale agreed in November 2018 to pay US $95 million to close a dispute in the United States over violations of anti-money laundering regulations. The settlement was part of a wider case in which the French bank agreed to pay US $1.34 billion to end US investigations over possible sanctions breaches (Reuters 2019).

REFERENCES

BIS. 2013. Fundamental review of the trading book: A revised market risk framework. Consultative Document, October, ISBN 92-9197-971-6.

———. 2017. Basel III: Finalising post-crisis reforms. December, ISBN 978-92-9259-022-2.

Draghi, M. 2018. Risk-reducing and risk-sharing in our Monetary Union. Speech at the European University Institute, Florence, May 11.

EBA. 2015. *EBA report on net stable funding requirements under article 510 of the CRR*. EBA/Op/2015/22, December 15.

EC. 2015. *Green Paper Building a Capital Markets Union*, COM/2015/063 final.

———. 2016a. Directive (EU) 2019/878 of the European Parliament and of the Council of 20 May 2019 amending Directive 2013/36/EU as regards exempted entities, financial holding companies, mixed financial holding companies, remuneration, supervisory measures and powers and capital conservation measures, June 7.

———. 2016b. Regulation (EU) 2019/876 of the European Parliament and of the Council of 20 May 2019 amending Regulation (EU) No 575/2013 as regards the leverage ratio, the net stable funding ratio, requirements for own funds and eligible liabilities, counterparty credit risk, market risk, exposures to central counterparties, exposures to collective investment undertakings, large exposures, reporting and disclosure requirements, and Regulation (EU) No 648/2012, June 7.

———. 2017a. Report from the Commission to the European Parliament and the Council on the Single Supervisory Mechanism established pursuant to Regulation (EU) No 1024/2013, Brussels, 11.10.2017, COM(2017) 591 final.

———. 2017b. Communication to the European Parliament, the Council, the European Central Bank, the European Economic and Social Committee and the Committee of the Regions on completing the Banking Union, COM(2017) 592 final. Brussels, October 11.

————. 2017c. Proposal for a Council Regulation on the establishment of the European Monetary Fund, Brussels, 6.12.2017 COM(2017) 827 final.

————. 2018. Amended proposal for a Regulation of the European Parliament and of the Council amending Regulation (EU) No. 1093/2010 establishing a European Supervisory Authority (European Banking Authority); Regulation (EU) No. 1094/2010 establishing a European Supervisory Authority (European Insurance and Occupational Pensions Authority); Regulation (EU) No. 1095/2010 establishing a European Supervisory Authority (European Securities and Markets Authority); Regulation (EU) No. 345/2013 on European venture capital funds; Regulation (EU) No. 346/2013 on European social entrepreneurship funds; Regulation (EU) No. 600/2014 on markets in financial instruments; Regulation (EU) 2015/760 on European long-term investment funds; Regulation (EU) 2016/1011 on indices used as benchmarks in financial instruments and financial contracts or to measure the performance of investment funds; Regulation (EU) 2017/1129 on the prospectus to be published when securities are offered to the public or admitted to trading on a regulated market; and (EU) Directive 2015/849 on the prevention of the use of the financial system for the purposes of money-laundering or terrorist financing, Brussels, 12.9.2018 COM(2018) 646 final.

————. 2019a. European Commission contribution to the European Council Capital Markets Union: Progress on building a Single Market for capital for a strong Economic and Monetary Union, March.

————. 2019b. Adoption of the banking package: Revised rules on capital requirements (CRR II/CRD V) and resolution (BRRD/SRM), Fact Sheet. Brussels, April.

EP. 2019a. Completing the Banking Union, In-depth analysis. Economic Governance Support Unit (EGOV), February.

————. 2019b. Loss-absorbing and recapitalisation capacity of credit institutions and investment firms (Directive), European Parliament legislative resolution of 16 April 2019 on the proposal for a directive of the European Parliament and of the Council amending Directive 2014/59/EU on loss-absorbing and recapitalisation capacity of credit institutions and investment firms and amending Directive 98/26/EC, Directive 2002/47/EC, Directive 2012/30/EU, Directive 2011/35/EU, Directive 2005/56/EC, Directive 2004/25/EC and Directive 2007/36/EC (COM(2016)0852 – C8-0481/2016 – 2016/0362(COD)).

————. 2019c. Loss-absorbing and recapitalisation capacity of credit institutions and investment firms (Regulation), European Parliament legislative resolution of 16 April 2019 on the proposal for a regulation of the European Parliament and of the Council amending Regulation (EU) No. 806/2014 as regards loss-absorbing and Recapitalisation Capacity for credit institutions and investment firms (COM(2016)0851 – C8-0478/2016 – 2016/0361(COD)).

FSB. 2015. Principles on loss-absorbing and recapitalisation capacity of G-SIBs in resolution total loss-absorbing capacity (TLAC) Term Sheet, November 9.

Lagarde, C. 2019. The euro area: Creating a stronger economic ecosystem. Suerf Policy Note, Issue 63.

Reuters. 2019. EU reviews Deutsche Bank, SocGen in screening of past money-laundering cases. *Business News*, June 6. https://www.reuters.com/article/us-eu-banks-moneylaundering/eu-reviews-deutsche-bank-socgen-in-screening-of-past-money-laundering-cases-idUSKCN1T71Y1.

Santander. 2017. Santander acquires popular, becoming the leading bank in Spain. Press Release (07/06/2017).

Sironi, A. 2018. *The evolution of banking regulation since the financial crisis: A critical assessment.* Baffi Carefin Centre Research Paper No. 2018-103.

CHAPTER 6

The Third Pillar of the Banking Union: The European Deposit Insurance Scheme

6.1 Introduction

This chapter addresses the legislative proposal made by the European Commission in November 2015 for introducing a European Deposit Insurance Scheme (EDIS). First, it investigates the role EDIS could play in helping to reassure depositors across the Banking Union and so reduce the risk of bank runs and increase financial stability. It would also enhance cooperation between national deposit insurance schemes (DISs) in responding to cross-border bank failures.

Then the chapter describes the Commission's proposal, which builds on national deposit insurance schemes and would be accessible only on the condition that commonly agreed rules have been fully implemented. European Union (EU) countries would start by filling up national Deposit Insurance Funds (DIFs), which would be financed by banks paying annual contributions that would amount to 0.8 per cent of all deposits covered by the scheme.

At the same time, banks would also have to contribute, separately, to the EDIS, which would gradually increase support to the national funds, in case they run out of money due to a bank failure. The Commission proposed that by 2024 the EDIS would completely take over the guaranteeing of all covered deposits in the euro zone from the national schemes, even though national funds would remain in existence.

© The Author(s) 2019   109
F. Arnaboldi, *Risk and Regulation in Euro Area Banks*, Palgrave
Macmillan Studies in Banking and Financial Institutions,
https://doi.org/10.1007/978-3-030-23429-4_6

In this framework, resolution and deposit insurance are strongly inter-connected. Following the European Commission proposal, a number of different recommendations have arisen in this area, but none of these options has met sufficient consensus among euro area countries, producing a deadlock in the policy discussion, with no apparent progress in the legislative discussion of the 2015 proposal itself. This chapter investigates the evolution of the third pillar after the approval of Directive 2014/49/EU.

6.2   Legislative Framework

Progress towards a common European financial framework has been a constant trend over the past 40 years, with ongoing harmonisation of national legislation and practices. The financial sector has played a key role in the integration of the European countries. Indeed, financial integration has been enhanced by the introduction of a single currency.

Despite the achievements in the integration of European financial markets and economies, the financial crisis confirms that closer coordination of prudential policies and safety nets is required. The European financial system has been revealed as being more fragile than expected. The crisis meant a serious setback for financial integration and the possibility of the break-up of the single currency.

As for the European retail banking markets, the financial crisis illustrated once more how banks are susceptible to the risk of bank runs and the need of a coordinated supervision at European level. Deposit insurance schemes help prevent such risk through the reimbursement of a limited amount of deposits to depositors whose bank has failed.

Directive 2014/49/EU set a uniform level of protection for depositors throughout the EU thanks to a broadened and clarified scope of coverage, faster repayment periods, improved information and robust funding requirements. However, it did not establish the third pillar of the Banking Union, a European Deposit Insurance Scheme (EDIS). At the beginning, it was decided to delay its creation and to opt instead for a harmonised network of national deposit insurance schemes (DISs).[1]

In 2015 progress towards the EDIS accelerated. The Five Presidents' Report (President of the European Commission, in close cooperation with the President of the Euro Summit, the President of the Eurogroup, the President of the European Central Bank and the President of the European Parliament [EP]) was published in July 2015 (Juncker et al. 2015). It sets out an ambitious programme of measures to underpin the economic and Monetary Union, among which is the EDIS. It will be applied alongside the Single Supervisory Mechanism (SSM) and the Single Resolution Mechanism (SRM) and be funded by risk-based contributions from banks operating in the Banking Union countries (FITD 2016).

In May 2015, in order to ensure consistent application of Directive 2014/49/EU and to provide incentives to banks to operate under a less risky business model, the European Banking Authority (EBA) issued guidelines to specify methods for calculating the contributions to DIS. In a context where many Member States did not have pre-financed DIS, the EBA set out principles for technically sound methods for calculating contributions to ensure that costs of deposit insurance are borne primarily by the banking sector (EBA 2015).[2]

The European Commission, in fulfilling a commitment, published in November 2015 a proposal for legislation, which sets out a euro area-wide e deposit insurance scheme for bank deposits and further measures to reduce remaining risks in the banking sector in parallel (EC 2015a). The legislative proposal proceeds through three successive stages: a reinsurance scheme for participating national DISs in a first period of three years; a co-insurance scheme for participating national DISs in a second period of four years; and full insurance for participating national DISs in the steady state, which starts in 2024 (EC 2015b) and is investigated in the next section.

6.3   European Deposit Insurance Scheme

6.3.1   November 2015 Commission Proposal

On 24 November 2015, the European Commission published a proposal to establish an EDIS. The proposal provides for the creation of a Deposit Insurance Fund (DIF) with a target size of 0.8 per cent of covered deposits in the euro area and the progressive mutualisation of its resources until a full-fledged scheme is introduced by 2024. The EDIS would be set up in three stages: first, for three initial years from July 2017 to July 2020, a reinsurance scheme would cover up to 20 per cent of the liquidity shortfall and up to 20 per cent of the excess loss of a participating DIS whenever pay-outs and losses exceed the DIS's available financial means. The liquidity would be provided through a loan which the DIS has to pay back, while the reinsured part of the excess loss, that is 20 per cent, would not have to be paid back.

Furthermore, in order to limit moral hazard, the reinsurance funding would be capped at the lowest between 20 per cent of the DIF's initial target level and ten times the target level of the insured DIS. In addition, the benchmark for calculating whether and to what extent a DIS can access the EDIS during the reinsurance phase is the hypothetical level of liquidity the DIS should have if it has complied with all its obligations, such as collecting *ex ante* contributions to reach the target level, and not the actual level of liquidity in a DIS (Carmassi et al. 2018). During the reinsurance stage, banks' risk-based contributions would be calculated with reference to the national banking system, that is relative to the riskiness of banks in the same country and not of all banks in the Banking Union.

In the second stage, for four years after the end of the reinsurance stage and until July 2024, a co-insurance scheme would be set up where the DIF would cover a gradually increasing share (20 per cent in year 1, 40 per cent in year 2, 60 per cent in year 3, 80 per cent in year 4) of the liquidity needs and losses of participating DISs. In the co-insurance stage, the intervention of the European scheme is independent of the national DISs' resources being exhausted. As in the reinsurance stage, the liquidity provided to the DIS would have to be repaid. Nevertheless, this is not the case for the covered loss, which would be shared pro rata between the national DISs and DIF in line with the gradually increasing coverage ratio. No cap would be provided for the amount due by the DIF. During the co-insurance stage, and differently from the reinsurance stage, banks' risk-based contributions would be calculated with reference to the riskiness of all banks in the Banking Union, that is at pan-European level.

In the third and final stage, starting in July 2024 (after the seven years of re- and co-insurance), a full insurance scheme would be in place: the EDIS would cover all liquidity needs and losses of participating DISs. In other words, the final stage consists of a 100 per cent mutualisation with national DISs being fully insured by the DIF. Furthermore, in this case there is no cap provided for the amount due by the DIF. To limit the potential moral hazard linked to a full EDIS, the Commission proposes that DISs can be disqualified from EDIS coverage if they do not comply with their obligations. As in the co-insurance stage, banks' risk-based contributions would be calculated taking into account the riskiness of all banks in the Banking Union. Table 6.1 summarises the main features of the three stages.

After the Commission's proposal, discussions in the European Parliament (EP) and the Council have revealed divergent positions as regards to the

Table 6.1 EDIS stages

	Reinsurance	*Co-insurance*	*Full insurance*
Period of time	3 years (2017–2020)	4 years (2020–2024)	>2024
Coverage	20% liquidity shortfall	20% in year 1, 40% in year 2, 60% in year 3, 80% in year 4	100%
	Up to 20 per cent of the excess loss	No cap	No cap
Intervention	The national DISs' resources must be exhausted	Independent of the national DISs' resources being exhausted	Independent of the national DISs' resources being exhausted
Pay back	Loan to be paid back on the liquidity shortfall No pay back on loss	Loan to be paid back on the liquidity shortfall Covered loss would be shared pro rata between the national DISs and DIF	Full insurance
Contribution	Reference to the national banking system	Reference to pan-European banking system	Reference to pan-European banking system

Source: Author's elaboration on EC (2015a)

design of the system at its final stage (reinsurance, co-insurance or full insurance), the timing of the setting up of such a system and the different degree of legacy issues and moral hazard risks present in the various national banking systems (EP 2016). Concerns have been expressed about the need to ensure that banks are sufficiently robust on a stand-alone basis, before sharing the potential burden of bank failures within the Banking Union.

6.3.2 European Parliament and ECOFIN Council's Position

On 4 November 2016, the rapporteur for the Commission's proposal in the European Parliament, Esther de Lange (EPP, Netherlands), presented her draft report (EP 2019). It supports a more cautious and conditional approach and changes the substance (only two stages of implementation) and the timeline of the Commission's proposal (2024 earliest). According to the de Lange's report, the DIF should amount to 0.8 per cent of covered deposits, as proposed by the Commission, but receive funding from the national and European level. The national DISs would remain in existence and, as from 2017, would provide half of the total funds in the European deposit guarantee scheme. Their financial means will rise continuously and reach the target funding level of 0.4 per cent of covered deposits in 2024. In addition to the national DISs, a euro area-wide DIF, made up of individual subfunds and a joint subfund, would be set up to provide the other half of the funds for deposit insurance. National DISs would need to be depleted first before making use of EU-level funding. The Commission's idea to make the nationality of banks irrelevant would thus become mitigated.

A reinsurance period would be introduced in 2019, while the second and final insurance phase would only be introduced when mandatory legally binding provisions have been passed on various parameters: the international standard for the Total Loss-Absorbing Capacity (TLAC) for global systemically relevant banks and the revised rules in relation to a Minimum Requirement for own funds and Eligible Liabilities (MREL) for all credit institutions affiliated to the participating DISs, which are addressed later in this chapter; an insolvency ranking for the subordinated debt of credit institutions, harmonised at EU level; a framework for business insolvency, harmonised at EU level, in relation to the early restructuring of companies in order to prevent and better handle the pressing issue of non-performing loans (NPLs); a leverage ratio for banks, including additional requirements for global systemically relevant banks (EP 2019).

More specifically, the reinsurance period (2019–2023) would start later than the Commission proposal and last one year longer. In contrast to the proposal, however, it provides up to 100 per cent of liquidity shortfall to participating DISs. As for the insurance period (as of 2024, earliest date possible), after fulfilling the conditions above, the European Commission would be empowered to adopt a delegated act to establish the exact date of application of the insurance period. In this final stage, an increasing level of excess loss of participating DISs will be covered, achieving 100 per cent coverage after five years. Funding that cannot be repaid with proceeds from insolvency proceedings does not have to be repaid.

The Parliament's Committee for economic and monetary affairs (ECON) held a discussion on the proposed amendments to the draft report on 25 January 2017. While the plenary vote had been initially scheduled for February 2017, the exchange of views on the draft report continues. On 29 March 2017, the Parliament's Committee on Constitutional Affairs (AFCO) adopted its opinion on the EDIS proposal (EP 2019).

The Council established an ad hoc working group in January 2016 to examine not only the EDIS proposal but also measures aimed at strengthening the Banking Union. The ECOFIN Council agreed on a roadmap to complete the Banking Union at its meeting on 17 June 2016. The idea is to start negotiations at the political level when the measures on risk-reduction are set and to choose an intergovernmental agreement when political negotiations on the EDIS start. In the ECOFIN Council of June 2016, ministers discussed a six-month report assessing progress in technical discussions on the EDIS.

To facilitate progress on the dossier, in its 2017 Communication, the Commission suggested to introduce the European Deposit Insurance Scheme in a more gradual manner, commensurate to progress achieved with regard to risk-reduction and the tackling of legacy issues, starting with a more limited reinsurance phase and moving gradually to co-insurance.

6.3.3 October 2017 Commission Communication

In October 2017 the European Commission published a Communication on the completion of the Banking Union (EC 2017), including a proposed new approach on EDIS aimed at addressing diverging views in the European Parliament and the Council. The European Parliament's own-initiative annual report on the Banking Union in 2017 recalled that the Banking Union remains incomplete, lacking an EDIS. In this respect, the Commission's communication of October 2017 was noted.

The Commission proposed to introduce the EDIS more gradually compared to its original proposal. During reinsurance, differently from the November 2015 proposal, there would be no coverage of losses, although the coverage of the liquidity shortfall would be higher, increasing progressively up to 90 per cent in the third year. By leaving losses to be covered nationally and providing liquidity assistance for national schemes if needed, this revised solution would safeguard depositor protection from the beginning (for which liquidity is needed) and take into account legacy and moral hazard concerns at the same time. The joint DIF, most likely managed by the existing Single Resolution Board and financed by contributions from banks, would be built up gradually.

The second stage would not start after a fixed number of years but would be contingent on a set of conditions to be assessed by the Commission, such as the reduction of banks' non-performing loans (NPLs) and Level 3 assets, described in the previous chapters. This set of conditions would include a targeted asset quality review (AQR) followed by the solution of the problems identified, such as active portfolio reductions. Such asset quality review should be conducted during the reinsurance phase, to ensure that legacy risks are addressed within the banking sectors where they were generated before the start of the co-insurance phase. This second phase would start only once these conditions are met. For instance, if the Commission proposes to set a threshold for NPL and L3 assets, banks not meeting the threshold would be required by supervisory authorities to prepare appropriate strategies on these issues.

If these conditions are met and co-insurance starts, the EDIS would also provide coverage for losses, starting with a 30 per cent coverage which should progressively increase. However, the Communication does not provide any information on how such an increase would take place and therefore the path of mutualisation is unclear. Depending on the end point of the progressive increase in losses coverage, the final stage could be closer to or more distant from full insurance. As the Communication indicated that the original proposal "remains on the table unchanged", it seems likely that full insurance in the steady state will be as initially drafted. Table 6.2 reports the main changes introduced by the Commission's 2017 Communication.

Table 6.2 EDIS stages—European Commission 2017 revision

	Reinsurance	*Co-insurance*	*Full insurance*
Period of time	3 or more years	Contingent on a set of conditions to be assessed by a Commission decision, which would include a targeted asset quality review (AQR) to address non-performing loans and Level III assets, followed by the solution of the problems identified (e.g. active portfolio reductions)	
Coverage	Up to 90% liquidity shortfall (30% in 2019, 60% in 2020 and 90% in 2021)	Full liquidity coverage	?
	No loss coverage	Losses: 30 per cent coverage which should progressively increase	
Intervention	The national DISs' resources must be exhausted		
Pay back	Loan to be paid back on the liquidity shortfall		

Source: Author's elaboration on EC (2017)

Recent debate has also considered different approaches to the EDIS, in particular referring to a possible design under which national DISs would intervene first, and the European Deposit Insurance Fund would only get involved subsequently. Despite some technical differences, the idea of national DISs or national compartments of the EDIS bearing the first burden is common across several proposals, such as the proposal by a group of French and German economists in January 2018 (Bénassy-Quéré et al. 2018). On this specific issue, Carmassi et al. (2018) investigate the potential impact and appropriateness of several features of the EDIS in the steady state. The main findings are the following: (1) a fully funded DIF would be sufficient to cover pay-outs even in a severe banking crisis; (2) risk-based contributions should account for specificities of banks and banking systems to address moral hazard and facilitate moving forward with risk-sharing measures towards the completion of the Banking Union in parallel with risk-reduction measures; (3) the analysis indicates that smaller and larger banks would not excessively contribute to the EDIS, their contribution being relative to the amount of covered deposits in their balance sheet, suggesting that measures to reduce contributions for the smallest and/or largest banks, as had been proposed by some Member States, would be unnecessary; (4) there would be no unwarranted systematic cross-subsidisation within the EDIS in the sense of some banking systems systematically contributing less than they would benefit from the DIF; and (5) the comparison between a full EDIS and a mixed deposit insurance scheme (where the national funds intervene before the European insurance fund) reveals that the latter would increase cross-subsidisation. This result is the consequence of some banking systems paying less under a mixed scheme, thus building up a smaller pool of resources because national target levels depend only on the amount of covered deposits and are thus risk-insensitive.

The Euro Summit on 29 June 2018 agreed that work should start on a roadmap for beginning political negotiations on the EDIS. Following on from the December 2018 Euro Summit, where a comprehensive package on strengthening the economic and Monetary Union was endorsed, the Eurogroup of 21 January 2019 exchanged views on the next steps on the EDIS, bringing the discussion to a more political level by establishing a high-level working group. This group will not be at a technical level, as happened up until 2018, and it will also be a more focused and less academic discussion. The group was given a broad mandate to take the EDIS forward and it is expected to report to the Eurogroup in June 2019.

6.3.4   Coordination with National Deposit Insurance Schemes

As indicated in EC (2015c), harmonisation of national deposit schemes needs to advance in parallel with the establishment of the EDIS to ensure the correct functioning of that scheme. Some important differences remain across Member States in the implementation of the Deposit Guarantee Scheme Directive rules, for example on the conditions to declare deposits unavailable, the eligibility of deposits, the financing of deposit guarantee schemes or the use of deposit guarantee scheme funds (EC 2017).

The exchange of information and instruments to promote coordination among national DISs also needs to be improved because for the EDIS to work properly, national competent authorities and deposit guarantee schemes will have to coordinate among themselves and with the Single Resolution Board, within very short notice. Adjustments to the Deposit Guarantee Schemes Directive are needed to facilitate cross-border interventions by such schemes, foster convergence and improve the exchange of information among national deposit guarantee schemes, competent authorities, the Single Resolution Board and the European Banking Authority. In particular, the role of the EBA should be designed to align the architecture of the three pillars of the Banking Union (supervision, resolution and deposit insurance). Indeed, in all three there will be a European Union central institution or an agency (the European Central Bank, the Single Resolution Board and the European Deposit Insurance Scheme, respectively) in charge of the implementation and a European Union agency (the EBA) coordinating national authorities operating in their respective fields.

6.3.5   Interaction Between the Pillars of the Banking Union

An issue related to the EDIS is its interaction with the requirement for TLAC introduced in 2015 by the Financial Stability Board (FSB) for global systemically important banks (G-SIBs) and the Minimum Requirement for own funds and Eligible Liabilities (MREL) introduced for all European and Banking Union banks by the BRRD (Bank Recovery and Resolution Directive) and the Single Resolution Mechanism Regulation (SRMR), respectively. As described in Chap. 5, the TLAC standard has been designed with the aim that failing global significant banks will have sufficient loss-absorbing and recapitalisation capacity available in resolution for authorities to implement an orderly resolution that minimises impacts on financial stability, maintains the continuity of critical functions and avoids exposing public funds to loss. The TLAC standard defines a minimum requirement for the instruments and liabilities that should be readily available for bail-in within resolution at global significant banks, but does not limit authorities' powers under the applicable resolution law to expose other liabilities to loss through bail-in or the application of other resolution tools (FSB 2015). The Minimum Requirement for own funds and Eligible Liabilities was first introduced by Directive 2014/59/EU with the aim of avoiding institutions excessively relying on forms of funding that are excluded from bail-in, since failure to meet the MREL would impact negatively on banks' loss absorption and recapitalisation capacity and, ultimately, the overall effectiveness of resolution (EC 2016).

Both the TLAC and MREL play a loss-absorbing function which, in principle, could protect the EDIS from losses related to resolution and enhance the resilience of the banking system in general. The amount of TLAC and MREL liabilities, in proportion to the overall bank balance sheet, as well as the amount of covered deposits in a bank will play a crucial role in determining whether the Deposit Insurance Fund would be effectively protected or should bear part of the losses in a bank resolution context (Carmassi et al. 2018). While the Deposit Insurance Fund is less likely to be involved in a resolution, it might still be possible, especially if a bank does not have sufficient loss-absorbing capacity and/or if the resolution authority decides to exercise its power to exclude on a discretionary basis some liabilities from the scope of bail-in, for example for financial stability purposes. This situation could possibly narrow the cushion of loss-absorbing capacity, which protects covered deposits/Deposit Insurance Funds. However, the possible intervention of the resolution fund, which is subject to certain preconditions and caps, would lower the probability of exposures of the Deposit Insurance Fund to losses (Carmassi et al. 2018).

Finally, the choice by the resolution authorities between resolving or liquidating a bank under an ordinary insolvency procedure will also play a crucial role: losses are likely to be higher under an insolvency procedure than in resolution, meaning that the Deposit Insurance Fund could be potentially more exposed to losses in insolvency than in resolution, although this depends on the loss-absorbing capacity of liabilities in resolution and liquidation. Anyway, the reverse cannot happen because losses for the Deposit Insurance Fund in resolution cannot be higher than under insolvency (Article 109.1 BRRD; Article 79.5 SRMR). All these elements have fundamental implications for the exposure of the DIF, which would be established under the EDIS.

As a final remark, if political issues are not swiftly resolved, the risk that the third pillar of the Banking Union remains undone is real. Without a true mutualized safety network, one of the main consequences that can be envisaged is related to potential differences in the costs of funding for large banking groups operating in different countries. Global banks may thus have incentives to move their headquarters to euro area countries where the cost of funding is lower (e.g. Luxembourg, Germany) or, alternatively, to set up holding companies located in these countries. In contrast, a European Deposit Insurance Scheme would increase customers' trust, as deposits would be reimbursed following common European rules, regardless of the country where the bank is incorporated. This would help break the link between banks and sovereigns in some countries. Furthermore, pooling resources at the Banking Union level would enhance the banking sector's resilience to shocks without leading to systematic transfers of risk between banking sectors. An EDIS would also remove the current misalignment among the three pillars of the Banking Union where supervision and resolution are regulated at the European level, while depositor protection remains a national task, reducing the likelihood of political interferences in banking business strategies.

6.4   CONCLUSION

The aim of completing the Banking Union has broad support and consensus in the European Union. The Eurogroup set out in July 2018 a detailed work programme for beginning political discussions on the EDIS. Following discussions at the Eurogroup between July and December, the 14 December 2018 Euro Summit agreed on the proposal of setting up a high-level working group to work on further steps on the EDIS, with a report expected by June 2019, reaffirming the importance of the Banking Union with a view to its completion.

After examining the major steps towards the completion of the Banking Union since Directive 2014/49/EU was passed, this chapter concludes that the EDIS would offer major benefits in terms of depositor protection while posing limited risks in terms of EDIS exposure since the probability and magnitude of interventions are likely to be low. The EDIS would also play a key role in terms of confidence building, also reducing the likelihood of bank runs. Additionally, results of Carmassi et al. (2018) show that there is no risk of unwarranted systematic cross-subsidisation. It is now time for the European Parliament and Member States to take political responsibility and agree on the necessary legal acts to complete the Banking Union.

NOTES

1. Further information can be found in "Germany Warns on Eurozone Bank Deposit Plan" (*Financial Times* 2015) and in the Deutsche Bundesbank's Monthly Report of December 2015, pp. 58–60.
2. Chapter 7 includes an empirical investigation by applying EBA guidelines to a sample of global systemically important banks.

REFERENCES

Bénassy-Quéré, A., M. Brunnermeier, H. Enderlein, E. Farhi, M. Fratzscher, C. Fuest, P. Gourinchas, et al. 2018. Reconciling risk sharing with market discipline: A constructive approach to euro area reform. CEPR Policy Insight No. 91, January.

Carmassi J., S. Dobkowitz, J. Evrard, L. Parisi, A. Silva, and M. Wedow. 2018. Completing the Banking Union with a European Deposit Insurance Scheme: Who is afraid of cross-subsidisation? ECB Occasional Paper Series 208, April 2018.

Deutsche Bundesbank. 2015. *Monthly report December 2015.*

Directive 2014/49/EU of the European Parliament and of the Council of 16 April 2014 on deposit guarantee schemes. *Official Journal of the European Union*, L 173/149.

EBA. 2015. Guidelines on methods for calculating contributions to deposit guarantee schemes. EBA/GL/2015/10, May 28.

EC. 2015a. Proposal for a Regulation of the European Parliament and of the Council amending Regulation (EU) 806/2014 in order to establish a European Deposit Insurance Scheme, Strasbourg, 24.11.2015, COM(2015) 586 final, 2015/0270(COD).

———. 2015b. Factsheet: A stronger banking union, November 24. http://ec.europa.eu/finance/general-policy/docs/banking-union/european-deposit-insurance-scheme/151124-factsheets_en.pdf.

———. 2015c. Communication from the Commission to the European Parliament, the Council, the European Central Bank, the European Economic and Social Committee and the Committee of the Regions "Towards the completion of the Banking Union", Strasbourg, 24.11.2015 COM(2015) 587 final.

———. 2016. Commission Delegated Regulation (EU) 2016/1450 of 23 May 2016 supplementing Directive 2014/59/EU of the European Parliament and of the Council with regard to regulatory technical standards specifying the criteria relating to the methodology for setting the minimum requirement for own funds and eligible liabilities, C/2016/2976.

———. 2017. Communication to the European Parliament, the Council, the European Central Bank, the European Economic and Social Committee and the Committee of the Regions on completing the Banking Union, COM(2017) 592 final, Brussels, October 11.

EP. 2016. European deposit insurance scheme completing the banking union, briefing EU legislation in progress, March 14.

———. 2019. JD – European Deposit Insurance Scheme (EDIS), legislative train, 05.2019, 5 deeper and fairer economic and monetary union.

Financial Times. 2015. Germany warns on Eurozone bank deposit plan, December 8.

FITD. 2016. *Annual report* 2015.

FSB. 2015. Principles on loss-absorbing and recapitalisation capacity of G-SIBs in resolution Total Loss-absorbing Capacity (TLAC) term sheet, November 9.

Juncker, J.-C., D. Tusk, J. Dijsselbloem, M. Draghi, and M. Schulz. 2015. *Completing Europe's economic and monetary union, July*. http://ec.europa.eu/priorities/sites/beta-political/files/5-presidents-report_en.pdf.

CHAPTER 7

The European Deposit Insurance Scheme

7.1 Introduction

This chapter empirically investigates the level of contribution banks must provide to a single deposit insurance scheme (DIS) according to their level of risk. The European Banking Authority (EBA) guidelines on methods for calculating contributions to a DIS (EBA 2015) are applied to a sample of global significant institutions (G-SII) at two different points in time: in 2014, before the Commission's proposal on a European Deposit Insurance Scheme (EDIS) described in Chap. 6, and in 2018, the last year with available accounting data on the EBA website. For the banks under scrutiny, core and additional indicators, as defined by the EBA (2015), are computed. Indicators belong to one of the following risk categories: capital, liquidity and funding, asset quality, business model and management, potential losses for the DIS.

The aim of this empirical investigation is to contribute to the regulatory debate by assessing which countries—if any—are better off after the full implementation of a common monitoring system of bank riskiness.[1]

7.2 The EBA Guidelines

Pursuant to Article 13(3) of the Directive 2014/49/EU of the European Parliament and of the Council of 16 April 2014 on deposit insurance schemes (DISs) (Directive 2014/49/EU), the EBA drafted guidelines on

© The Author(s) 2019   123
F. Arnaboldi, *Risk and Regulation in Euro Area Banks*, Palgrave
Macmillan Studies in Banking and Financial Institutions,
https://doi.org/10.1007/978-3-030-23429-4_7

the methods for calculating contributions to deposit insurance schemes (DISs). Before the guidelines' approval, many Member States did not have pre-financed DIS. Hence the guidelines set out principles for technically sound methods for calculating contributions to ensure that costs of deposit insurance are borne primarily by the banking sector and that the available financial means reach the target level within the time horizon envisaged in Directive 2014/49/EU.

The EBA (2015) aim is to provide incentives to banks to operate under a less risky business model. To that end, the guidelines set out principles on the risk component of the calculation method. In addition, they capture various aspects of the banks' risk profile by specifying a number of core risk indicators pertaining to capital, liquidity and funding, asset quality, business model and management and potential losses for the DIS. In line with the principle of proportionality, the guidelines allow domestic authorities to take into account the diversity of banks and business models while respecting a number of safeguards inherent in the need for harmonisation and comparability within the euro area.

The guidelines allow authorities to set aside, with regard to a given type of institution, a core risk indicator that is unavailable due to the legal characteristics of such banks or supervisory regime in which they operate. The authorities may introduce additional risk indicators, provided that the minimum weights specified for the remaining core indicators and risk categories are respected. The authorities also have a margin of flexibility, allowing them to reshuffle up to 25 per cent of indicators' weights in order to increase the importance of risk indicators that better capture differences in risk profiles. In any event, the weight of any additional indicator, or any increase in the weight of a core indicator, may not exceed 15 per cent, except for qualitative indicators in the risk category "Business model and management", where full flexibility is allowed in order to properly reflect the diverse characteristics of banks. The guidelines offer a unique opportunity to assess progress in the convergence of national practices in calculating contributions to DIS from 2014, the year before their introduction, and 2018, the last year with available accounting data.

7.3   MONITORING SYSTEM OF BANK RISKINESS

7.3.1   Risk Indicators

The EBA guidelines have been applied to a sample of global systemically important institutions (G-SIIs) and other large institutions with an overall exposure measure of more than 200 billion euros at the end of each year. The EBA list comprises 36 banks in 2018 incorporated in 11 European Union countries. For the purpose of this chapter, euro area countries are considered, that is 7 out of 11 countries, and 23 out of 36 banks.[2] Accounting data are downloaded from Orbis Bank. Table 7.1 reports the list of banks in the sample.

Descriptive statistics on core and additional indicators for the final sample of 23 banks are reported in Table 7.2.

Table 7.1   Sample banks

Country	Bank	Number of banks	Sample percentage
Austria	Erste Group	1	0.04
Belgium	Kbc	1	0.04
France	Banque Postale	6	0.26
	Bnp Paribas		
	Credit Agricole		
	Bpce		
	Credit Mutuel		
	Societe Generale		
Germany	Bayern Lb	5	0.22
	Commerzbank		
	Deutsche Bank		
	Dz Bank		
	Lbbw		
Italy	Intesa Sanpaolo	2	0.09
	Unicredit		
Netherlands	Abn Amro	3	0.13
	Ing		
	Rabobank		
Spain	Santander	5	0.22
	Bbva		
	La Caixa		
	Sabadell		
	Bfa		

Source: Author's elaboration on EBA (2018)

Table 7.2 Descriptive statistics

Indicators (in percentage)	All years					2014					2018				
	No. of observations	Mean	Standard deviation	Min	Max	No. of observations	Mean	Standard deviation	Min	Max	No. of observations	Mean	Standard deviation	Min	Max
Core															
Leverage ratio	41	0.048	0.010	0.030	0.070	21	0.045	0.010	0.030	0.066	20	0.050	0.010	0.036	0.070
CET 1 ratio	40	0.128	0.019	0.093	0.184	20	0.122	0.016	0.093	0.153	20	0.135	0.020	0.109	0.184
Capital coverage ratio	40	0.031	0.005	0.021	0.043	21	0.029	0.004	0.021	0.036	19	0.033	0.004	0.028	0.043
Liquidity ratio	44	0.229	0.100	0.040	0.480	23	0.201	0.106	0.040	0.453	21	0.259	0.086	0.121	0.480
NPL ratio	43	0.052	0.041	0.010	0.179	23	0.068	0.048	0.011	0.179	20	0.034	0.020	0.010	0.088
Return on asset	44	0.003	0.003	-0.006	0.010	23	0.002	0.003	-0.006	0.007	21	0.004	0.003	0.000	0.010
RWA to total asset	40	0.348	0.083	0.231	0.555	20	0.350	0.093	0.231	0.555	20	0.345	0.072	0.255	0.515
Additional															
Return on equity	44	0.056	0.047	-0.099	0.135	23	0.043	0.053	-0.099	0.133	21	0.070	0.034	0.005	0.135
Total asset growth	44	0.021	0.052	-0.099	0.148	23	0.033	0.060	-0.099	0.148	21	0.008	0.038	-0.086	0.073
Cost to income	44	0.662	0.105	0.427	0.927	23	0.649	0.111	0.427	0.862	21	0.676	0.098	0.536	0.927

Source: Author's elaboration on Orbis Bank data and on EBA (2015)

7.3.2   Core Indicators

For the first risk category (capital), the EBA proposes two core indicators: leverage ratio, defined as tier 1 capital to total asset ratio, and capital coverage ratio (actual to required CET1 ratio) or common equity tier 1 ratio (common equity tier 1 capital to risk weighted assets [RWA]). Capital indicators reflect the level of the loss-absorbing capacity of the bank. Higher amounts of capital show that the bank has a better ability to absorb losses internally, thus decreasing its likelihood of failure. Therefore, banks with higher values of capital indicators should contribute less to the DIS (EBA 2015). In the sample, the leverage ratio is on average 5 per cent and the CET1 12.8 per cent, considering both 2014 and 2018. Both ratios increased from 2014 to 2018, reflecting an improved banks' solidity. Similar considerations can be drawn on the capital coverage ratio, the overall average of which is equal to 3.1 per cent.

For the liquidity and funding category, the two core indicators suggested by the authority (liquidity coverage ratio—LCR—and net stable funding ratio—NSFR) cannot be applied because, even if their definition as determined in Regulation (EU) No 575/2013 is fully operational, few data are available on Orbis Bank. As a transitional indicator, the liquidity ratio (LR) defined as liquid assets to total assets is computed. It measures the bank's ability to meet its short-term debt obligations as they become due. The higher the ratio, the larger the safety margin to meet obligations and unforeseen liquidity shortfalls. Indeed, low liquidity levels indicate the risk that the institution may be unable to meet its current and future, expected or unexpected, cash-flow obligations and collateral needs. Liquid assets cover 23 per cent of total assets on average and increased from 20 per cent in 2014 to 26 per cent in 2018. Even if two Spanish banks score an LR below 5 per cent in 2014, and two other banks have an LR below 10 per cent in 2014, LR is higher than 10 per cent for all banks in 2018, thus indicating that possible future liquidity tensions have been solved.

The asset quality category shows the extent to which the bank is likely to experience credit losses. Large credit losses may cause financial problems that increase the likelihood of failure, therefore justifying higher contributions to the DISs. This category includes the non-performing loan (NPL) ratio, given by NPLs to total assets. It provides an indication of the type of lending the bank engages in. A high degree of credit losses in the loan portfolio indicates lending to high-risk customers. The NPL ratio is on average 5.2 per cent, considering both years. From 2014 to 2018, the ratio decreased from 6.8 to 3.4 per cent, on average. Only four banks show a ratio higher than 15 per cent in one of the years under scrutiny (three banks in 2014, one bank in 2018). Among those banks, two are Italian and two are Spanish institutions.

Business model and management takes into account the risk related to the bank's current business model and strategic plans and reflects the quality of internal governance and controls. Business model indicators can, for instance, include indicators related to profitability, balance sheet development and exposure concentration. The first core indicator proposed by the EBA is risk weighted assets-to-total-assets ratio, which indicates the kind of risky activities a bank engages in. A higher value indicates higher risk. A second core indicator is return on asset (ROA). A business model that is able to generate high and stable returns indicates lower risk. However, unsustainably high levels of ROA also indicate higher risk (EBA 2015). In the sample, risk weighted assets (RWA) to total assets ratio is 34.8 per cent on average, decreasing from 2014 to 2018. It is, however, larger than 50 per cent for four Spanish and one Austrian bank in 2014 and for two banks in 2018, raising doubts on the sustainability of their business model. ROA is on average equal to 0.03 per cent and increasing over the four-year period. Two banks have a negative value of ROA in 2014. The maximum value of ROA in the sample is one per cent, and this does not seem unsustainably high.

The last risk category is potential losses for the DIS. The EBA (2015) suggests one core indicator (unencumbered assets to covered deposits), which measures the degree of expected recoveries from the bankruptcy estate of the bank, which was resolved or put into normal insolvency proceedings. A bank with a low ratio exposes the DIS to higher expected loss. However, the proposed definition of unencumbered asset does not allow the ratio to be computed.[3]

7.3.3   Additional Indicators

In addition to the core risk indicators, DISs may include additional risk indicators that are relevant for determining the risk profile of member banks. The additional risk indicators should be classified into the above-listed risk categories. The EBA proposes indicators for the asset quality, business model and management and potential losses for the DIS categories. In this empirical investigation, three additional indicators belonging to the business model and management category are applied: (1) excessive balance sheet growth ratio (total asset growth—TAG), which measures the growth rate of the bank's balance sheet. Unsustainably high growth might indicate higher risk; (2) return on equity (ROE), which measures the ability to generate profits to shareholders from the capital these have invested in the bank. A business model that is able to generate high and stable returns indicates reduced likelihood of failure. However, unsustainably high levels of ROE indicate higher risk; (3) cost-to-income ratio (CI), which measures cost-efficiency. An unusually high ratio may indicate that the institution's costs are out of control, especially if represented by the fixed costs (i.e. higher risk). A very low ratio may indicate that operating costs are too low for the institution to have the required risk and control functions in place, also indicating higher risk (EBA 2015).

The mean of the sample for total asset growth is 2.1 per cent and it goes from 3.3 per cent in 2014 to 0.8 per cent in 2018. However, 15 banks have a negative asset growth at least in one year (7 banks in 2014 and 8 banks in 2018—of which one bank is common to both years); two banks have a TAG ratio larger than 10 per cent in 2014. These banks show high total asset growth, which indicates higher risk.

On average, ROE is equal to 5.6 per cent with an increasing trend over the four-year period and it is negative for two banks in 2014. The EBA (2015) states that unsustainably high levels of profitability ratios also indicate higher risk. The maximum value of ROE in the sample is 13.5 per cent, which does not suggest particular problems of the sustainability of the business model in the long term.

On the efficiency side, the average cost-to-income ratio is 66.2 per cent. From 2014 to 2018 this ratio in fact increased from 64.9 to 67.6 per cent. Two German and one French bank have a ratio larger than 80 per cent at least in one year: in particular the two German banks have a ratio larger than 80 per cent in both 2014 and 2018. The high ratio indicates that the bank's costs could be more adequately controlled. A very low ratio may indicate that operating costs are too low for the bank to have the required risk and control functions in place, also indicating higher risk, but this is not the case for the sample under scrutiny since only two Spanish banks have a CI ratio smaller than 50 per cent in 2014, and this value cannot be considered as critical (EBA 2015).

Overall this chapter examines 7 out of 9 core indicators and 3 out of 13 additional indicators.

7.4   INDIVIDUAL RISK SCORE

As is normal practice, the EBA proposes thresholds, classes and weights to compute individual bank risk scores (IRS). The EBA allows two methods to assign banks to risk classes: the bucket method and the sliding method. The first one uses a fixed number of buckets defined for each risk indicator by setting upper and lower boundaries for each bucket. The number of buckets for each risk indicator should be at least two. The buckets should reflect different levels of risk posed by the member banks (e.g. high, medium, low risk) assessed on the basis of particular indicators (EBA 2015).

Where the calculation method follows the sliding scale approach instead of a fixed number of risk classes, the upper and lower limits are set by the DIS on the basis of regulatory requirements or historical data on the particular indicator. Since the sliding method is based on information available only to the national DIS, this empirical investigation employs the bucket method.

7.4.1   Bucket Method

In the bucket method, an IRS is assigned to each bucket. The buckets' boundaries should be determined either on a relative or absolute basis. When using the relative basis, the IRSs of banks depends on their relative risk position vis-à-vis other institutions; in this case, institutions are distributed evenly between risk buckets, meaning that institutions with similar risk profiles may end up in different buckets. In the absolute basis, the buckets' boundaries are determined to reflect the riskiness of a specific indicator; in this case, all banks may end up in the same bucket if they all have a similar level of riskiness.

For each risk indicator, the IRSs assigned to buckets should range from zero to 100, where zero indicates the lowest risk and 100 the highest risk. Table 7.3 shows an example of bucket scoring by type of risk indicator, where higher values of the risk indicator mean higher risk (e.g. NPL ratio).

To compute the IRS of the sample banks, buckets and boundaries provided by the EBA have been used for the NPL ratio, ROA, ROE and TAG. The EBA does not provide specific examples for the leverage ratio, CET1, LR, RWA-to-total assets (TA) ratio and cost-to-income ratio; thus relative boundaries, which correspond to the 20th, 40th and 60th percentiles of the sample banks distribution year-to-year, have been used for those indicators. The percentiles and corresponding IRS have been fixed according to EBA guidelines. Relative boundaries imply an even distribution of banks among risk buckets, and Table 7.4 shows an example of buckets, relative boundaries and IRS.

Table 7.3 Buckets, boundaries and individual risk score

Buckets	Boundaries	IRS
1	<2%	0
2	=<2%–7%<	50
3	>=7%	100

Source: EBA (2015)

Note: Risk indicator for which higher values indicate higher risk (NPL ratio)

Table 7.4 Buckets, relative boundaries and individual risk score

Bucket	Boundaries	IRS
1	>60° percentile	0
2	<40°–60°=<	33
3	<20°–40°=<	66
4	=<20° percentile	100

Source: Author's elaboration on EBA (2015)

Note: Risk indicator for which higher values indicate lower risk (liquidity ratio)

7.4.2   Aggregate Risk Score

The EBA (2015) multiplies each IRS by an indicator weight (IW), which should be the same for all banks and calibrated by using supervisory assessment and/or historical data on failures of institutions (EBA 2015).

The sum of weights assigned to all risk indicators is equal to 100 per cent. When assigning weights to particular risk indicators, the minimum weights for the risk categories and core risk indicators, which sum up to 75 per cent, should be preserved, as specified in Table 7.5 column (a).

Table 7.5 column (b) shows the weights assigned to risk indicators when only core indicators are computed and NSFR is not yet available. The EBA (2015) states that the minimum IW assigned to NSFR is assigned to LR, which belongs to the same risk category. Table 7.5 column (c) shows one of the possible allocations of weights suggested by the EBA when both core and additional indicators are computed. In particular, the regulator's proposal allows five additional indicators in four different categories. These indicators can be freely chosen by the DIS.

Table 7.5, columns (b) and (c), shows the allocation of the flexible 25 per cent of weights among core and additional indicators (EBA 2015).

Table 7.5   Risk categories, indicators and IW

Risk categories and risk indicators	Minimum IW (%)	Core	Core + additional
Column	(a)	(b)	(c)
Capital	18	24	23
Leverage ratio	9	12	9
Capital coverage ratio to CET1	9	12	9
Additional risk indicator 1			5
Liquidity and funding	18	24	18
Liquidity ratio	9	24	9
Net stable funding ratio (NSFR)	9	Na	9
Asset quality	13	18	18
NPL ratio	13	18	13
Additional risk indicator 2			5
Business model e management	13	17	23
RWA/total asset	6.5	8.5	6.5
ROA	6.5	8.5	6.5
Additional risk indicator 3			5
Additional risk indicator 4			5
Potential losses for the DIS	13	17	18
Unencumbered asset/covered deposits	13	17	13
Additional risk indicator 5			5
Total	75	100	100

Source: EBA (2015)

The aggregate risk score (ARS) is the weighted average of the IRS, according to the following formula:

$$ARS_i = \sum_{j=1}^{n} IW_j * IRS_j \tag{7.1}$$

where

$$\sum_{j=1}^{n} IW_j = 100\%$$

and

$$IRS_j = IRS_{xj} \text{ when } X \text{ in } \{A,B,...,M\},$$

that is the bucket corresponding to indicator A_j

Following the guidelines, since NSFR is not computed during the transition period, the IWs listed in Table 7.5 column (b) are applied to core indicators. In addition, as previously mentioned, the ratio of unencumbered assets to covered deposits has not been computed because data on unencumbered assets for the sample banks are not available. Thus, the weight (17 per cent) originally assigned by the EBA to this ratio is equally allocated among all other computed indicators.

Consequently, when only core indicators are investigated, the ARS is computed according to:

$$ARS_{core} = 0.15 * \text{leverage ratio} + 0.15 * CET1 + 0.25 * LR$$
$$+ 0.21 * NPL\,\text{ratio} + 0.12 * RWA\,/\,TA + 0.12 * ROA \qquad (7.2)$$

When core and additional indicators are considered, the weights shown in Table 7.5, column (c), are applied to each risk category, except for the business model and management. All three additional indicators belong to this category, thus its weight is given by the sum of the weights of business model and management and of potential losses for the DIS.

$$ARS_{core+additional} = 0.115 * \text{leverage ratio} + 0.115 * CET1 + 0.18 * LR$$
$$+ 0.18 * NPL\,\text{ratio} + 0.085 * RWA\,/\,TA + 0.085 * ROA$$
$$+ 0.08 * ROE + 0.08 * TAG + 0.08 * CI \qquad (7.3)$$

Table 7.6 reports the descriptive statistics of ARS computed by applying formulas (2) and (3) to the sample banks.

Though the averages of ARS_{core} and $ARS_{core+additional}$ are very similar, which is 49 versus 50 when all years are considered, 53.7 versus 54.2 in 2014 and 43.4 versus 45.6 in 2018, the $ARS_{core+additional}$ standard deviation is lower than ARS_{core} in all time periods considered. This may suggest a lower volatility of the aggregate risk score when additional indicators are taken into consideration.

According to the EBA (2015), every ARS has a corresponding aggregate risk weight (ARW), which should be used to calculate the contribution of an individual member bank to the DIS (Table 7.7).

When ARW is 75 per cent, the member bank gets a discount on the contribution to be paid because it is considered as a low risk bank. When ARW is 100 per cent, the contribution does not change. When ARW is higher than 100 per cent (either 125 or 150 per cent), the member bank is considered as a high-risk bank and has to pay higher contributions.

Table 7.6   Aggregate risk score by year

Indicators	Number of observations	Mean	Standard deviation	Minimum	Maximum
All years					
ARS$_{core}$	38	48.81	15.54	21.12	85.00
ARS$_{core+additional}$	38	50.11	12.03	27.02	84.50
2014					
ARS$_{core}$	20	53.66	15.06	23.10	85.00
ARS$_{core+additional}$	20	54.25	11.74	33.33	84.50
2018					
ARS$_{core}$	18	43.43	14.62	21.12	72.85
ARS$_{core+additional}$	18	45.52	10.87	27.02	63.89

Source: Author's elaboration on Orbis Bank data

Table 7.7   Aggregate risk weight

Risk classes	ARS boundaries	ARW
1	<40	75%
2	=<40–55<	100%
3	=<55–70<	125%
4	>=70	150%

Source: EBA (2015)

Table 7.7 shows that the average ARS of the sample banks is about 49, which assigns the sample to the ARW of 100 per cent. Overall, banks' contributions to the national DIS do not change when risk is assessed. Similar considerations apply if 2014 and 2018 are separately investigated: even if both aggregate risk weights are lower in 2018 than in 2014, the assigned weight is 100 per cent overall.

Table 7.8 shows the aggregate risk scores by country.

Austrian, Belgium and Italian banks are assigned, on average, to the ARW of 125 per cent. Overall, banks incorporated in those countries should pay higher contributions to the national DIS. German, French and Dutch banks, on the contrary, are assigned to the 100 per cent weight. Spanish banks should be assigned to the riskiest weight if only core indicators are considered. They switch to the 100 per cent weight if core and additional indicators are used to compute the aggregate risk score. The choice between aggregate risk scores is not neutral: when additional

Table 7.8 Aggregate risk score by country

Country	Indicators	N. of observations	Mean	Standard deviation	Minimum	Maximum
Austria	ARS$_{core}$	2	66.10	26.73	47.20	85.00
	ARS$_{core+additional}$	2	64.97	27.62	45.44	84.50
Belgium	ARS$_{core}$	1	62.95	.	62.95	62.95
	ARS$_{core+additional}$	1	58.94	.	58.94	58.94
Germany	ARS$_{core}$	9	40.57	14.08	21.12	64.05
	ARS$_{core+additional}$	9	44.48	10.42	31.35	61.48
Spain	ARS$_{core}$	5	57.49	6.04	53.85	67.90
	ARS$_{core+additional}$	5	53.81	4.93	48.88	60.09
France	ARS$_{core}$	11	45.97	13.73	23.10	66.21
	ARS$_{core+additional}$	11	49.46	10.53	33.33	64.38
Italy	ARS$_{core}$	4	66.70	7.47	58.00	73.00
	ARS$_{core+additional}$	4	62.47	5.86	55.14	69.28
Netherlands	ARS$_{core}$	6	39.13	11.98	21.75	57.10
	ARS$_{core+additional}$	6	42.01	10.28	27.02	55.67

Source: Author's elaboration on Orbis Bank data

indicators are included, banks incorporated in Austria, Belgium, Spain and Italy improve their score on average, whereas banks in France, Germany and the Netherlands result in being riskier, on average. Even if in this assessment the change in scores does not imply a change in weights—with the only exception of Spanish banks—this could be the case when all indicators are considered by the regulators.

ARS is not assigned at country level but to each member bank year by year: additional information is reported in Table 7.9.

Table 7.9 part (a) lists the number of banks in each risk class using only core indicators in year 2014 and 2018 for all euro area banks included in the sample; part (b) shows the distribution of banks considering both core and additional indicators.

Looking at core indicators (Table 7.9 part (a)) from 2014 to 2018, the number of banks in risk class 1 increases by 270 per cent, whereas the number of banks in class 2, 3 and 4 (ARW = 100 per cent) decreases (−7, −75 and −44 per cent, respectively). Thus, it seems that the sample banks became less risky over the four-year period, and their contributions to the DIS could be lower. Table 7.9 part (b) confirms this trend, applying core and additional indicators to sample banks in year 2014 and year 2018. The number of banks in class 1 increases by 233 per cent, and the number of

Table 7.9   Number of banks, risk classes, ARW_{core} and $ARW_{core+additional}$ (2014 and 2018; all countries)

		2014		*2018*		
Risk classes	ARW_{core}	Number of banks	Percentage	Number of banks	Percentage	Change 2014–2018 (%)
1	75%	3	0.15	10	0.56	2.70
2	100%	6	0.30	5	0.28	−0.07
3	125%	9	0.45	2	0.11	−0.75
4	150%	2	0.10	1	0.06	−0.44
	Total	20	1	18	1	
Risk classes	$ARW_{core+additional}$	Number of banks	Percentage	Number of banks	Percentage	Change 2014–2018 (%)
1	75%	2	0.10	6	0.33	2.33
2	100%	8	0.40	8	0.44	0.11
3	125%	9	0.45	4	0.22	−0.51
4	150%	1	0.05	0	0.00	−1.00
	Total	20	1	18	1	

Source: Author's elaboration on Orbis Bank data

banks in class 2 increases by 11 per cent. The number of banks in class 3 is cut by a half (−51 per cent) and the only bank assigned to the riskiest class (class 4) migrates to class 3, leaving the riskiest class empty (−100 per cent).

Table 7.10 reports the number of banks in each risk class using core and core plus additional indicators in year 2014 and 2018 by each euro area country in the sample.

When core indicators are investigated, all countries report a shift of banks to less risky classes, with the only exception being Italian banks, which overall keep the same class (class 3 and 4, higher contributions to DIS), even if, in fact, the two banks switched their positions.

As previously noted, when core and additional indicators are both investigated, the situation slightly differs. For instance, among French banks, three banks move from the less risky class to riskier classes. One German bank out of four (25 per cent) does not pay lower contributions to the scheme, but keep the 100 per cent aggregate risk weight. The same applies to one Spanish bank out of the three in the sample. On the contrary, both Italian banks are assigned to a lower risk class (class 3), and not to class 3 and 4. The situation remains unchanged only for Austrian and Dutch banks.

Table 7.10 Number of banks, risk classes, ARW_{core} and $ARW_{core+additional}$ (2014 and 2018; by country)

Country	Risk classes	ARW_{core}	2014	2018	$ARW_{core+additional}$	2014	2018
			Number of banks			Number of banks	
Austria	1	75%	0	0	75%	0	0
	2	100%	0	1	100%	0	1
	3	125%	0	0	125%	0	0
	4	150%	1	0	150%	1	
		Total	1	1	Total	1	1
Belgium	1	75%	0		75%	0	
	2	100%	0		100%	0	
	3	125%	1		125%	1	
	4	150%	0		150%	0	
		Total	1	0	Total	1	0
Germany	1	75%	2	4	75%	1	3
	2	100%	1	0	100%	2	1
	3	125%	2	0	125%	2	0
	4	150%	0	0	150%	0	
		Total	5	4	Total	5	4
Spain	1	75%	0	0	75%	0	0
	2	100%	0	3	100%	1	2
	3	125%	2	0	125%	1	1
	4	150%	0	0	150%	0	
		Total	2	3	Total	2	3
France	1	75%	1	3	75%	1	0
	2	100%	3	1	100%	3	4
	3	125%	2	1	125%	2	1
	4	150%	0	0	150%	0	
		Total	6	5	Total	6	5
Italy	1	75%	0	0	75%	0	0
	2	100%	0	0	100%	0	0
	3	125%	1	1	125%	2	2
	4	150%	1	1	150%	0	
		Total	2	2	Total	2	2
Netherlands	1	75%	0	3	75%	0	3
	2	100%	2	0	100%	2	0
	3	125%	1	0	125%	1	0
	4	150%	0	0	150%	0	
		Total	3	3	Total	3	3

Source: Author's elaboration on Orbis Bank data

Table 7.11 Risk indicators and aggregate risk scores before and after Directive 2014/49/EU

Indicators (in percentage)	No. of observations	Mean	No. of observations	Mean	Difference in means
	Pre directive		Post directive		
Core					
Leverage ratio	21	0.45	20	0.05	0.4*
CET 1 ratio	20	0.122	20	0.135	−0.013**
Capital coverage ratio	21	0.029	19	0.033	−0.004***
Liquidity ratio	23	0.202	21	0.259	−0.057**
NPL ratio	23	0.068	20	0.034	0.034***
Return on asset	23	0.002	21	0.004	−0.002***
RWA to total asset	20	0.35	20	0.345	0.005
Additional					
Return on equity	23	0.043	21	0.07	−0.027**
Total asset growth	23	0.033	21	0.008	0.025*
Cost to income	20	0.65	18	0.676	−0.026
Aggregate risk score					
ARS$_{core}$	20	53.664	18	43.425	10.239**
ARS$_{core+additional}$	20	54.249	18	45.515	8.734**

Source: Author's elaboration on Orbis Bank data

Note: The table reports the descriptive statistics (number of observations, mean values and differences in means) for the risk indicators for euro area countries where Directive 2014/49/EU was implemented during the sample period 2014–2018. *, ** and *** indicate significance at 10%, 5% and 1% levels, respectively

As a final remark, Table 7.11 reports the univariate analysis of the risk indicators and aggregate risk scores pre- and post-adoption of Directive 2014/49/EU.

Results should be interpreted with caution, as the sample is very small. On average, the level of loss-absorbing capacity of euro area G-SIIs significantly improved from 2014 to 2018. Both the CET1 and capital coverage ratio are significantly higher at 5 and 1 per cent level, respectively. The tier 1 to total asset ratio is however lower, even if at lower significance level (10 per cent). Liquidity is significantly higher and the NPL ratio lower, suggesting the efficacy of the NPL reforms euro area countries passed in this four-year period. Even if ROA is still quite low, it significantly improved between 2014 and 2018, from 0.2 to 0.4 per cent, on average.

Additional indicators all seem to suggest an improvement in the business model and management of banks. The balance sheet growth ratio is significantly lower (from 3.3 to 0.8 per cent at 10 per cent level), indicating a sustainable growth rate of total assets. Return on equity is significantly higher, thus reporting a greater ability to generate profits to shareholders from the capital these have invested in the bank. A business model that is able to generate high and stable returns indicates reduced likelihood of failure.

As for the risk scores, both the ARS_{core} and the $ARS_{core+additional}$ are significantly lower after the implementation of Directive 2014/49/EU at 5 per cent level. Even if both scores are still in the second risk class, they are now closer to the lower boundary, suggesting that further improvements in banks' risk may lead, on average, to a change of class and to the assignment of a 75 per cent weight. In the end, this would determine a discount on contribution to be paid. This chapter contributes to the literature on banking supervision by investigating the third pillar of the Banking Union, that is deposit insurance schemes, a matter on which the use of information has been limited in order to prevent such use from affecting the stability of the banking system or depositor confidence (Directive 2014/49/EU art. 16 c.5).

The EBA guidelines offer a basis on which to assess progress in the convergence of national practices in calculating contributions to DISs with the aim of understanding whether G-SII banks would be negatively affected by their implementation, fuelling systemic risk, as opined by some member countries.

Germany, the EU's biggest economy, does not want its depositors to be liable for pay-outs in the event of bank failures elsewhere. It insists the EU must first take steps to minimise risks before starting talks on shared responsibility. Berlin insisted that any reference to setting up such a deposit scheme be removed at the EU summit in October, and has succeeded in doing so again at the December meeting (Reuters 2015).

In fact, the EBA proposal would increase the number of banks in the lower risk classes, where the contribution quota to the DIS would remain unchanged or would decrease. The view that national concerns should be overcome to find an agreement on DIS is increasingly supported by regulators:

In sum, we need a European banking system that can *bend* in a storm without breaking, we need a banking system that will truly diversify risks across the ecosystem and irrigate growth. It is clear what is left to be done: establish common deposit insurance. We can find ways to resolve our legitimate national concerns and plant that vital shade-tree. I want to emphasize that this system will be *funded by banks*, not taxpayers. To get this done, member countries will need to agree on a mutually acceptable balance between risk-sharing and risk-reduction—between *trust* and *accountability*. This will not be easy. But today I *urge* euro area leaders to reignite the discussion, to negotiate in good faith and make the difficult compromises, to unlock the full potential of the banking union. (Lagarde 2019)

7.5   Conclusion

In the last few years the euro area banking sector has continued to reduce its level of risk, benefitting from the positive macroeconomic developments in most euro area countries and from the implementation of several reforms both at the EU and at the national level. After having described the three main sources of risk for the euro area banks (Chaps. 2, 3 and 4) and the steps towards completing the Banking Union (Chaps. 5 and 6), this chapter empirically investigates the level of risk of a sample of G-SII euro area banks selected by the European Banking Authority in its annual assessments. To this aim, the monitoring system of bank riskiness proposed by the EBA (2015) is employed by applying risk indicators, scores and weights.

Overall, this assessment suggests a reduced riskiness of the sample banks after the implementation of the Directive 2014/49/EU and of the domestic and European reforms described in the previous chapters. Differences among euro area countries persist, but they partially depend on the set of risk indicators used by the regulatory authority. The methods for calculating risk-based contributions to national DIS should properly address the characteristics of the national banking sectors and business models of member institutions with the goal to reduce the potential losses stemming from a DIS intervention by adequately reflecting the likelihood of the bank's failure. A wider set of indicators may help to calibrate contributions to each country's banking system specificity.

The EBA (2015) guidelines were incorporated in the domestic supervisory processes and procedures by the end of 2015, with the exception of Latvia, Poland and Finland. From that date on, and in any case no later than by 31 May 2016, contributions to be raised by national DISs comply with these guidelines, de facto creating national deposit insurance schemes working under the same European rules.

NOTES

1. This chapter describes only the indicators used in the empirical investigation and refers to EBA (2015) for further details on the complete list of risk categories and indicators.
2. Denmark, Norway, Sweden and the United Kingdom have been excluded as they do not participate in the euro area.
3. EBA defines unencumbered and encumbered assets as the following: "an asset should be treated as encumbered if it has been pledged or it is subject to any form of arrangement to secure, collateralise or credit-enhance any on-balance sheet or off-balance sheet transaction from which it cannot be freely withdrawn (for instance, to be pledged for funding purposes)" (EBA 2015, p. 22).

REFERENCES

Directive 2014/49/EU of the European Parliament and of the Council of 16 April 2014 on deposit guarantee schemes, *Official Journal of the European Union*, L 173/149.

EBA. 2015. Guidelines on methods for calculating contributions to deposit guarantee schemes. EBA/GL/2015/10, May 28.

———. 2018. EBA global systemically important institutions' (G-SIIs) data disclosure exercise. https://eba.europa.eu/risk-analysis-and-data/global-systemically-important-institutions/2018.

Lagarde, C. 2019. The Euro Area: Creating a Stronger Economic Ecosystem. SUERF Policy Note Issue No 63, April.

Reuters. 2015. EU deposit insurance vanishes from EU leaders' draft conclusions, December 18. http://uk.reuters.com/article/uk-eurozone-banks-deposits-idUKKBN0U11KP20151218.

INDEX[1]

[1] Note: Page numbers followed by 'n' refer to notes.

© The Author(s) 2019
F. Arnaboldi, *Risk and Regulation in Euro Area Banks*, Palgrave
Macmillan Studies in Banking and Financial Institutions,
https://doi.org/10.1007/978-3-030-23429-4

143

Printed by Printforce, the Netherlands